Translator Self-Training Program

English-into-French

Workbook

Schreiber Publishing

Rockville, MD

Third Printing
ISBN 978-1-887563-05-5

Acknowledgement: Section 2, Assignment 4, and Section 3, Assignment 4 are used with the kind permission of the World Bank.

Printed in the U.S.A. by Schreiber Publishing, PO Box 4193, Rockville, Maryland 20849
301/725-3906 1-800-953-9929

Table of Contents

SECTION 1. GENERAL

INTRODUCTION

Welcome to *Schreiber's* **Translator Self-Training Program**. We are very pleased you selected this program, which has been in use since 1992. It has helped aspiring translators around the country get their start in this exciting field, while assisting practicing translators in improving their translation skills. Translation is one of the fastest growing professions in today's world, as different languages and cultures are coming closer together every day. Whether you wish to pursue translation full-time or as a sideline, you will find it to be a highly challenging and quite profitable occupation. The purpose of the following exercises is to help you improve your skills as an English-into-French translator.

This program is designed to help you work at your own pace and gain experience through translation practice assignments. These assignments, excerpted from actual translation jobs, were selected to help you determine your own level of comfort and expertise, so that you may go on from there to choose the type of translation work you might like to pursue.

To derive the maximum benefit from these texts, you should carefully read the General Comments, the guidelines, and the specific notes which discuss each assignment. Every comment and every guideline represents years of experience in professional translation work. By carefully following this program, you will be able to achieve *in just a few days* what has taken others years to learn. You will be guided through many of the pitfalls of translation, taught how to avoid them, shown shortcuts in accomplishing a complex piece of translation work, and be given the benefit of comments designed to show you how to produce a translation acceptable to major clients such as government, industry, the legal world, and many more.

Before you read further, we strongly urge you to read the following chapters in the book *Guide for Translators,* included in this kit:

Chapter 3: Basic Requisites for Becoming a Professional Translator
Chapter 4: The Well-Rounded Translator
Chapter 5: Good and Bad Translation Habits
Chapter 6: Translation Techniques
Chapter 7: Translation Equipment
Chapter 8: Dictionaries and Reference Literature

The above-listed chapters will give you a good overview of how translation work is to be approached and practiced. Try to keep the contents of these chapters in mind as you translate the following assignments.

You are presented with four different texts which, for most people, represent an increasing level of difficulty (although if you happen to be a lawyer, for example, it is possible that you will find the second assignment the easiest of the four). They are:

1. **General**
2. **Legal**

3. **Chemical/Medical**
4. **Business/Finance**

At a minimum, you may want to do the first and second assignments. Those two represent a vast body of material which is being translated in the United States on a regular basis, but which does not require a highly specialized vocabulary or technical background. The third assignment requires access to chemical and medical terminology, which can be managed by any intelligent translator. The fourth assignment should be approached with caution. Here one must have an understanding of the world of finance, which not all of us do. For your own self-assessment, you may want to try it (since we provide you with the translation, you can compare the results and see for yourself how you did). But if you find it too difficult, don't be discouraged. It is clearly not for everyone.

We hope you enjoy working with these texts, and we urge you to please be patient with yourself. One does not become an accomplished translator overnight. To learn, one must make mistakes. If your heart is in it, and if you love the challenge of working with two languages you happen to know well, then you are sure to get a great deal out of this program.

A Word about French Translation

French, once the language of international diplomacy and the favorite of cultivated people everywhere, is still today one of the world's major languages in nearly every field of human endeavor. It is one of the leading languages in both Europe and Africa, the second language of Canada, the language of Caribbean nations like Haiti, and it is widely studied in many countries around the world.

Many American college students choose French for their foreign language requirement, or even major in this language. From all indications, given the popularity of the French language and the continued economic and cultural importance of France, French should continue to play a significant role on the international scene in the next century.

This means that developing one's skills as a English-into-French or French-into-English translator is time well spent. The United States and France continue to interact in all areas of commerce, science and technology. Documentation and literature flow between the two countries and between the U.S. and other French-speaking parts of the world in a steady stream and in both directions. As the global village becomes more of a reality with every passing day, the interaction between French and English intensifies, and requires an ever-growing volume of translation in real time.

Some maintain that in time English will replace other languages such as French, Spanish, German, etc. and will become the one language used by everyone in all international activities. Such claims were made in the past - in the time of the Roman Empire, for example. The fact remains, however, that at any given time in history there were always multiple cultural centers in the world, and even here in the United States, where English has been the dominant language for at least two centuries, other languages are gaining importance, and cultural pluralism, rather than disappearing, is flourishing.

The following exercises are designed to help you achieve a worthy and profitable goal - becoming an expert in improving communications between two of the world's major cultures and tongues - English and French.

GENERAL COMMENTS

The following comments are offered with two purposes in mind: the immediate purpose is to help you with the assignments. The long-term purpose is to serve as reference material for actual translation work. Keep them for future use.

A reminder:
The "source language" is the language you translate from.
The "target language" is the language you translate into.

Every language has its own "personality," so to speak. When you translate, pretend you are two different persons - an "English Person" and a "French Person." The English Person reads the original English text, and becomes familiar with it. The English Person then turns to the French Person, and says to him/her, "**Okay, now it's your turn to say the same thing your way**." Now the French Person takes over, and starts writing the same text in French. You will be constantly switching back and forth between the English and the French Persons, as the first checks the English word, phrase, sentence structure, and then the second thinks in French and comes up with the right equivalents. Here are some of the main language issues you will have to deal with:

Clarity

We each have our own personal style of expressing ourselves - in any language. Some people make their point clearly and succinctly, while others use more words than necessary, including esoteric words, to make their point. The same holds true in translation. You can translate the phrase, "It's a matter of taste" as "chacun à son goût," or as "des goûts et des couleurs on ne discute pas." In the first instance, only four words were used; in the second, nine. Most of the time, the first type of translation is better, because it is simpler and more readily understandable. Make it your point to pursue simplicity whenever possible.

Consistency

Most of the time, if you start out translating the word "house" as "maison," stick to "maison," and don't start suddenly shifting to "bâtiment," or vice versa. The reader may become confused, wondering why the word suddenly changed. Bâtiment is generally bigger than maison, and one may wonder whether the dimensions of that particular structure might have changed. If you are familiar with word-processing you know how easy it is to do a "global search and replace" throughout the text, so that if halfway into the document you decide that "bâtiment" is better than "maison," then go back to the beginning and do a global change, replacing the word "maison" with "bâtiment."

Sentence Structure

It is difficult, yet very important, to ensure that sentence structure is correct and makes sense, yet still retains the flavor of the original text, particularly if this is written in a flowery, elaborate, or otherwise unique style. This fine line is achieved mainly through practice, but it is definitely helpful to read the original several times before even beginning the translation process in order to gain a good idea of the author's style.

It is not necessary to follow the structure of a sentence literally. A run-on sentence which may make sense in one language may not make sense in the other, and therefore should be divided into two sentences (or more). The converse is also true. You should also avoid being too literal when it comes to word order, or your text will sound stilted, awkward, and artificial. You will need to rely on your own good writing skills in determining the most sensible word order and punctuation so that your translation flows smoothly.

Format

Format should be followed as closely as possible. Ideally, every page of translation should look exactly like the corresponding page of the original, except, of course, for the language. There is a very practical reason for this It helps the reader, who may or may not know the source language, compare the two texts, make sure all the parts are there, and check a particular word or phrase in the source text. This, however, is not always possible, since a page of translation at times is longer than the same page in the source language. Nevertheless, every effort should be made to keep the format as similar as possible to the original.

Terminology

The use of the right terminology is critical in any translation, especially in any technical subject. Here the right kind of dictionaries and reference literature becomes very critical. Keep in mind, however, that dictionaries, no matter how good, are never complete, and do not provide all the answers. The other source of information is people who work in the field the particular translation covers. Their input is often more valuable than that of the dictionary, since they are the ones who work in the field and represent the potential readers of your translation.

The first thing to keep in mind about terminology - as was discussed before - is consistency. If you translate a word a certain way, do not change in the middle of the text to another synonym of the same word, even though it may be accurate. This will throw the reader off. The second thing is to make sure you are using the right terms, rather than trying to approximate them. Keep a list of those terms to maintain consistency throughout the document, and also for future use. If you continue to translate in the same technical field, these lists will become your most valuable translation tool.

Acronyms

When an acronym appears in the text, it is good to establish a rule of thumb depending on the particular document. If the acronym represents a familiar institution or organization, one with a known French equivalent (for example, NATO, or OTAN in French), then it is okay to translate it into French. On the other hand, if the text refers to a U.S. company, such as IBM, it would not make sense to translate it into French, and it should be left as IBM. Obviously, it would not help anyone if IBM (International Business Machines) were translated as MCI (machines commerciales internationales), which would be confused with the phone company of the same initials.

Numbers

The use of commas and periods is reversed in numbers over 1000 (1,000 in English is 1.000 in French), and in decimals (0.5 in English becomes 0,5 in French). This is one example of cultural differences which must be closely observed.

Punctuation

Quotation marks are appropriate in English, but this is not always so in French. Semicolons have their place in both languages, but not necessarily in the same places. These are just a few examples of how even a highly accurate translation will not always mirror its original text. You will often be called upon to be the judge, which involves a combination of excellent writing skills, knowledge of rules of grammar and punctuation, plus common sense.

Errors in the Source Text

Sometimes you will find that the original has errors, such as a misspelling where it is clear by the context that the author intended to say "one" and not "on," or the sequence in a series of numbered clauses is wrong, or a name that has been in upper case letters suddenly appears as lower case, for no apparent reason. You can do a number of things in situations such as these. You can go ahead and make the correction and leave it at that. You can translate the text as is, and use the term [sic] after the error, to alert the reader. Or you can make a translator's note on a separate sheet of paper. Ultimately, the client will have to decide what to do with it.

Untranslatable Words or Terms

You may run into a word, a term or a phrase which cannot be translated, or which should be left in the original language (such as, for instance, "rock and roll"). If there is a need to explain it, it can be done in a footnote or in parentheses (or brackets, which makes it clearer that the bracketed text is not part of the original) following the word (rock and roll [musique de danse très populaire]). As a general rule, however, it is best not to burden your translation with footnotes or parenthetic or bracketed text.

In Conclusion

The above notes are by no means exhaustive. They do not cover all the issues facing a translator. Language is not mathematics. Keep this in mind, and do the best translation job you possibly can.

GUIDELINES FOR TRANSLATING THE ASSIGNMENTS

1. We are providing you with an English text and a French translation of that same text. Pretend you don't have the French translation. If you read it before you do the assignment, you will not be able to do an honest job, and you will not derive the benefit of learning from your own mistakes.

2. Read the English text once for general comprehension. Underline any difficult words or passages.

3. As you start the translation process by reading the text for the first time (see 2., above), keep track of time, so that when you finish you will know how long it took you to translate the text. This is very critical, because you want to increase your translation speed as you go along. The rule is simple: the more words you translate per hour, the more money you will make. A very low hourly word-count can earn you less than minimum wage, which is not at all desirable. (Note: The hours indicated at the top right hand corner for each assignment include two numbers. The first is for beginners while the second number is for an experienced translator. Therefore, an assignment that would take a beginner 5-7 hours to complete might take an experienced translator 2 hours. The timeframe includes research, draft, and final copy.)

4. Read it again. This time make a list of difficult words, and make any notes regarding things you need to clarify about the text (e.g., look up something in an encyclopedia to better understand some concept or piece of information).

5. Try to determine which dictionaries and reference books you need for this assignment, get hold of them, and keep them nearby.

6. Now you are ready to start translating. Preferably, you will be using a computer. If this is too intimidating, write it out the first time. It will take longer, but you will have more time to think. Remember, your objective is to translate on computer, not in longhand. These days, if you want to earn money translating, you have to submit text on disk. There are hardly any exceptions to this requirement.

7. Do a draft translation. Go over the draft. Do the best you can to make the French sound like good, clear, correct French which does not sound like English and does not retain any English forms in either style, format, or any technical points. Be sure you did not omit anything. Ask yourself if you succeeded in conveying the correct sense of every idea and every word in the source text. Be sure you are comfortable with every single word you chose in French, and that you have no doubts or hesitations. If, after all this, you do have some questions, do not worry. No one expects you to do perfect work the first time around. You will do better next time.

8. Now that you have accomplished your translation, figure out the time it took you to reach your

final version (including all the previous steps, namely first reading, research, draft, and final copy).

9. Make a list of the words, passages, and concepts in the text where you encountered difficulty, and keep for future reference. This kind of record keeping will help you improve your performance, and serve as a reminder not to repeat the same mistake twice.

10. Print out your corrected and edited text.

GUIDELINES FOR SELF-EVALUATION

1. Turn to the French translation in Section 3, and compare it to yours. Next read the notes concerning the pitfalls and salient points of this text very carefully, and see how they compare to your own experience with the text. They may not necessarily coincide with everything you experienced personally, but they do provide you with some tips on the do's and don'ts of technical translation.

2. The most important thing for you to keep in mind as you compare your translation to the one in Section 3, is that there is no one absolutely correct way of translating a text. Many words can be translated in more than one way. Many sentences can be structured in more than one way. Many ideas can be conveyed in different words. In fact, your translation may turn out to be just as good, and in some spots even better than the one in the book.

3. Keep track of the shortcomings of your translation. The areas you are interested in are the following:

   Omissions - did you fail to translate any particular word or phrase, or even paragraph?

   Format - does your format follow the original (breaking into paragraphs, for instance)?

   Mistranslations - did you mistranslate any particular word?

   Unknown words - were there any words you were not able to translate?

   Meaning - did you miss the meaning of any particular phrase or sentence?

   Spelling - did you misspell a word?

   Grammar - did you make any grammatical mistakes?

   Punctuation - did you mispunctuate or miss any punctuation marks?

   Clarity - did you fail to clearly convey the meaning of any particular part of the text?

   Consistency - did you call something by one name, and then by another without good reason?

   Cognates - were you "tripped" by a word in the source text, whereby you mistranslated it because it looked the same, though it changes meaning in the target language (for instance, the word "actual"["actuel"] exists in both English and French, but means two different things)?

   Style - are you satisfied with the way your translation reflects the style of the original (for example, the original is written in a clear, direct style, while the translation sounds complex and indirect)?

These are some of the questions you have to ask yourself. As you go on to translate other texts, always keep these questions in mind as you self-assess your translation. By improving your performance in the above areas, you are on your way to becoming an accomplished translator.

SECTION 2. ASSIGNMENTS

6-7/2.5 hours

ASSIGNMENT 1: GENERAL

Cote d'Ivoire's Experience with a Concession for Water Supply

An excellent example of a private company providing public services in West Africa is Cote d'lvoire's SODECI. SODECI is an Ivorian company whose capital (about $15 million) is owned 52 percent by local interests; 46 percent by Saur, the French water distributor; and 2 percent by a government investment fund. It started operations with the Abidjan water supply system thirty years ago and now manages more than 300 piped water supply systems across the national territory. Until recently, SODECI operated under concession contract for water production in Abidjan, the capital city. It was under lease contract for water production and distribution in all other urban centers; for water distribution in Abidjan; and for management of the Abidjan sewerage system.

To deal with financial troubles caused by government policies in the 1980s regarding sectoral investment and tariffs, the urban water sector was reorganized. SODECI's contract for urban water supply services was transformed into a concession contract for the entire country, with SODECI taking responsibility for both operations and investments. Today the company has 300,000 individual connections that serve some 70 percent of Cote d'lvoire's 4.5 million urban residents - 2 million in Abidjan and the rest in settlements of 5,000 to 400,000 people. Under a policy to provide low-income households with direct access to water, 75 percent of SODECI's domestic connections have been provided with no direct connection charge. The number of connections is growing between 5 and 6 percent a year.

Since the early 1970s, full cost recovery has been the rule, and revenues from water sales have fully covered capital and operation and maintenance costs. During the past ten years, unaccounted-for water has never exceeded 15 percent, and collection from private consumers has never fallen below 98 percent (collection from government agencies is more problematic). Moreover, despite the dispersion of operations, there are only four staff per thousand connections, reflecting best practice standards. The company has also succeeded in reducing expatriate staff while expanding operations.

SODECI retains part of the rates collected to cover its operating costs, depreciate its assets, extend and rehabilitate distribution networks, and pay dividends to shareholders. It also pays the government a rental fee to service the debt attached to earlier projects financed by the government.

SODECI provides service close to the standards of industrial countries. Yet the cost to consumers is no higher than in neighboring countries in similar economic conditions or in members of the CFA franc zone, where tariffs rarely cover capital and operation and maintenance costs, and service lags behind. Private Ivorian interests now own a majority of SODECI's shares. Its bonds are one of the main items traded on Abidjan's financial market, and it has distributed dividends to its shareholders. The company has also paid taxes since its inception.

Success of a Lease Contract - Guinea's Water Supply

When the Republic of Guinea's water supply sector was restructured in 1989, it was one of the least developed in West Africa. At that time a new autonomous water authority, SONEG, took over ownership of the urban water supply infrastructure and assumed responsibility for sector planning and investment. SEEG, 49 percent government-owned and 51 percent owned by a foreign consortium, was created to operate and maintain the system's facilities.

Under the ten-year lease contract signed with SONEG, SEEG operates and maintains the system at its own commercial risk. Its remuneration is based on user charges actually collected and fees for new connections. SEEG also benefits from improvements it achieves in the collection ratio, from reduced operating costs, and from reductions in unaccounted-for water. Since SONEG has ultimate responsibility for capital financing, it has strong incentives to seek adequate tariffs and to make prudent investments based on realistic demand forecasts.

To make sure the necessary tariff increases would be affordable, the Guinean lease contract included an innovative cost-sharing arrangement. Under the agreement negotiated by the government, the two sector entities, and the external financier (the World Bank), the consumer tariff was to be adjusted gradually from the first to the tenth year of the contract. During this period the World Bank agreed to assume a declining share of the foreign exchange expenditures of operation, and the central government covered a declining share of the debt service. By the tenth year tariffs were expected to cover the full cost of water. Tariff increases have to date exceeded the planned schedule, rising from $0.12 per cubic meter in 1989 to about $0.75 in 1993. Despite higher tariffs, the collection ratio for private customers has increased dramatically - from less than 20 percent to more than 75 percent in 1993-and technical efficiency and service coverage have improved.

Tailoring Concessions to Sectors and Government Objectives

The method of awarding concessions or the right to operate is extremely important in determining the incentives to private sponsors. When the returns to the sponsor are unrelated - or only weakly related - to the performance of the operation, the benefits of private sponsorship are foregone.

The goal is to ensure an attractive financial return for investors while safeguarding public interests. One key element of negotiation is the price the investor pays for the right to operate the service - or the extent of capital or operating subsidy that the government may provide. Other negotiating points are the price that will be charged for services, the concession period, and the rights and obligations at the end of the contract period.

This is a complex brew, with each element depending on another. There is always a danger that the terms of a concession will allow investors to secure too high a rate of return, or will fail to provide sufficient incentives for proper maintenance of the assets and provision of services.

To simplify matters, certain norms and conventions have been adopted. The length of concession periods is typically related to the life of the underlying asset. For example, thirty-year concessions are common for toll roads, and fifteen years is common for power generation projects (although for hydroelectric projects, thirty years is more likely). Contracts for solid-waste disposal are in the range of four years, a period in which garbage trucks depreciate considerably. But because trucks can be sold more easily than assets underlying roads and power plants, the contract period may be as short as several months.

An interesting variation is used in telecommunications, although it could also be applicable for independent power projects. The focus is not on the length of the concession period, which can be indefinite, but on the period of the exclusive concession. In Mexico and Argentina, the newly privatized companies have been granted exclusive licenses for six to ten years, during which they have certain investment obligations. After the exclusive period, the government is free to allow new entrants.

The method of charging for the right to provide service can take different forms. In theory, it is most efficient to award a concession to the bidder who offers the largest lump sum up front. Having paid a large initial fee, the operator will be motivated to operate the facility in the most efficient manner. For large projects, however, where project costs and revenues are uncertain, revenue sharing or profit-sharing arrangements can spread the risk (as in the Guangzhou-Shenzen highway in China). Where the government sees itself mainly as a guardian of consumer interest, it may choose to receive no fee but to award the contract on the basis of the lowest price charged to the consumer (which can later create problems with quality of service and requires specification of minimum service standards).

word count: 1243

6-7/2.5 hours

ASSIGNMENT 2: LEGAL

AGREEMENT

BETWEEN: NOVA INVESTMENTS, INC.

AND: SAFE MANAGEMENT LIMITED

ARTICLE I
INTRODUCTION

1. 1. Date and parties to the agreement. This AGREEMENT, dated 12 May 1994, has been reached between Nova Investments, Inc. (THE CUSTOMER) a Canadian company, and Safe Management Limited (SAFE), a Canadian corporation.

1. 2. Goal of the agreement. This AGREEMENT establishes the terms and conditions under which the Customer has retained the services of SAFE to manage and operate the Food Service for the clientele: the employees, visitors and tenants of the Customer in the facilities (premises) of the Customer located at 1000 Boulevard Etoile, Quebec, H7V 3X8. The term "Food Service" as used in this AGREEMENT describes the operation of conventional facilities to provide food, beverages and other products that the Customer might authorize.

1.3. Duration of the agreement. The initial duration of this AGREEMENT is for two (2) years, beginning 1 June 1994 and is renewable on an annual basis, until one of the parties terminates it according to the conditions provided below.

ARTICLE 4
MANAGEMENT AND PERSONNEL

4.1. The employees of SAFE. SAFE must provide a sufficient number of employees who are qualified at the management level and staff for good operation of the Food Service. These employees will be supervised by the support and management staff of SAFE. All personnel hired by SAFE must at all times and in all duties be in the exclusive employment of SAFE. The initial understandings pertaining to salary negotiations and other conditions will be the understandings which are reached between the two parties.

SAFE will directly pay its employees.
4.2. Hiring policy agreement.

a) SAFE undertakes to recruit, train, manage, guide, discipline and if necessary dismiss personnel working in the Food Service.

b) The Customer may not hire, enter into agreements or allow the hiring for its own food services, any management personnel of the SAFE Food Service before one (1) year passes following termination of his employment with SAFE or before one (1) year following termination of this AGREEMENT.

c) The Customer will have the right to inspect management personnel.

ARTICLE 8
GENERAL TERMS AND CONDITIONS

8.1. Taxes. SAFE will collect all taxes which are applied and will remit these taxes to the pertinent agencies. The water bill and business taxes will be paid for by SAFE.

8.2. Legal provisions. SAFE must adhere to the applicable laws, ordinances, . regulations and rules of the federal, provincial, municipal and local government bodies, offices and administrations in charge of sanitation, safety and health of the Food Service and must procure and maintain all necessary licenses and permits. The Customer will provide all necessary assistance to SAFE in its efforts to procure and obtain this conformity.

8.3. Responsibility for general insurance. SAFE must obtain and keep in force during the time period of this AGREEMENT general insurance against bodily injury and property damage for the combined limit of not less than one million dollars ($1,000,000) including, but not limited to, responsibility for all bodily injury, contractual responsibility and responsibility for losses of product, covering only the operations and activities of SAFE which are stipulated in the present AGREEMENT. SAFE will provide to the Customer the certificates indicating the insurance policies which cover operation under this AGREEMENT. The insurance policy must include a clause of the issuing company to the effect that the policy will not be canceled unless a written notification is given to the Customer at least thirty (30) days in advance.

8.4. Recovery waiver. Each of the parties to this AGREEMENT renounces according to mutual agreement all their rights as well as rights of their branches and affiliates to obtain compensation from the other party for losses or damages to buildings, improvements or other property caused by fire, explosion or by any other cause normally included in a standard insurance policy or a policy covering fire, bodily injury, or civil responsibility. The Customer will protect his building including the Food Service area, its contents and other insured properties against losses or damage from fire, explosion and damages of that kind.

OPERATING AGREEMENT
Between
TELECOM-FRANCE and
U.S. TELEPHONE

FOR THE PROVISION OF DIGITAL PRIVATE LINE TELECOMMUNICATIONS SERVICES

1. TELECOM-FRANCE and U.S. TELEPHONE hereby agree to interconnect operating facilities in order to provide customers with digital private line services via SATELLCOM WBS. These services will be developed in accordance with existing C.C.I.T.T. recommendations and the appropriate SATELLCOM WESS documentation.

2. Agreement for any equipment to be provided directly to TELECOM-FRANCE by U.S. TELEPHONE will be via attachment to this agreement.

3. Under this agreement, each of the parties will be responsible for providing the segment of the communications link from the customer's premise in its respective country to the Atlantic region midpoint; that is, in the U.S.A., U.S. TELEPHONE will be responsible for the telecommunications segment between the customer's premises and the satellite; in Cote d'Ivoire, TELECOM-FRANCE will be responsible for the telecommunications link between the customer's premises and the satellite. These segments, however, will be technically and operationally compatible with each other in order to provide the desired services.

4. TELECOM-FRANCE and U.S.TELEPHONE will make separate and independent arrangements with the customer, and each will establish the rates and conditions under which its portion of the service will be provided. However, TELECOM-FRANCE and U.S.TELEPHONE will exchange tariffs and other marketing information. TELECOM-FRANCE and U.S. TELEPHONE will enact One-Stop Shopping and Single End Billing arrangements at the request of and on behalf of individual customers. Where appropriate, other arrangements may also be used by mutual agreement of the parties. In the event of a service interruption, there will be nonfinancial obligation between TELECOM-FRANCE and U.S. TELEPHONE. However, each of the parties will give interruption allowances to the customer for the period of time when the service is unavailable in accordance with the terms and conditions of their respective tariffs applicable to the particular service.

5. Points of contact in both TELECOM-FRANCE and U.S. TELEPHONE will be designated; names of these persons will be exchanged to ensure the operational integrity of the services offered.

6. Other terms and conditions may be added to the agreement from time to time as they may be mutually agreed upon by TELECOM-FRANCE and U.S. TELEPHONE.

Signed for and on behalf of	Signed for and on behalf of
U.S.TELEPHONE	TELECOM-FRANCE
Signature:_______________	Signature:________________
Name:_________________	Name:________________
Title:__________________	Title:__________________
Date:_______________	Date:_________________

word count: 1059

ASSIGNMENT 3: CHEMICAL/MEDICAL

NAME OF DRUG

CURITOL®

(Levocarnitine)

THERAPEUTIC CLASSIFICATION

Replenisher (Carnitine)

ACTION AND CLINICAL PHARMACOLOGY:

CURITOL® (Levocarnitine) is a naturally occurring substance required in mammalian energy metabolism. It has been shown to facilitate long-chain fatty acid entry into cellular mitochondria, therefore delivering substrate for oxidation and subsequent energy production. Fatty acids are utilized as an energy substrate in all tissues except the brain. In skeletal and cardiac muscle they serve as major fuel. Primary systemic carnitine deficiency is characterized by low plasma, RBC, and/or tissue levels. It has not been possible to determine which symptoms are due to carnitine deficiency and which are due to the underlying organic acidemia, as symptoms of both abnormalities may be expected to improve with carnitine. The literature reports that carnitine can promote the excretion of excess organic or fatty acids in patients with defects in fatty acid metabolism and/or specific organic acidopathies that bioaccumulate acyl CoA esters.

Secondary carnitine deficiency can be a consequence of inborn errors of metabolism. CURITOL® may alleviate the metabolic abnormalities of patients with inborn errors that result in accumulation of toxic organic acids. Conditions for which this effect was demonstrated are: Glutaric aciduria II, methyl malonic aciduria, propionic acidemia, and medium chain fatty acyl CoA dehydrogenase deficiency. Autointoxication occurs in these patients due to the accumulations of acyl CoA compounds that disrupt intermediary metabolism. The subsequent hydrolysis of the acyl CoA compound to its free acid results in acidosis that can be life threatening. Levocarnitine clears the acyl CoA compound by formation of acyl carnitine which is quickly excreted. Levocarnitine deficiency is defined biochemically as abnormally low plasma levels of free carnitine, less 20 μM/L at age greater than one week post term and may be associated with low tissue and/or urine levels. Further, this condition may be associated with a ratio of plasma ester/free levocarnitine levels greater the 0.4 or abnormally elevated levels of esterified levocarnitine in the urine. In premature infants and newborns, secondary deficiency is defined as plasma free levocarnitine levels below age related normal levels.

INDICATIONS AND CLINICAL USAGE:

CURITOL® (Levocarnitine) Oral Solution (1 g/10 mL Multidose), 330 mg Tablet and Injection (1 g per 5 mL):

CURITOL® (Levocarnitine) is indicated in the treatment of primary systemic carnitine deficiency. In the reported cases, the clinical presentation consisted of recurrent episodes of Reye-like encephalopathy, hypoketotic hypoglycemia, and/or cardiomyopathy. Associated symptoms included hypotonia, muscle weakness and failure to thrive. A diagnosis of primary carnitine deficiency requires that serum, red cell and/or tissue carnitine levels be low and that the patient does not have a primary defect in fatty acid or organic acid oxidation (see Clinical Pharmacology). In some patients, particularly those presenting with cardiomyopathy, carnitine supplementation rapidly alleviated signs and symptoms. Treatment should include, in addition to carnitine, supportive and other therapy as indicated by the condition of the patient.

CURITOL® (Levocarnitine) is also indicated for acute and chronic treatment of patients with an inborn error of metabolism that results in a secondary carnitine deficiency.

CONTRAINDICATIONS:

None known.

WARNINGS:

None.

PRECAUTIONS:

General:

CURITOL® (Levocarnitine) Oral Solution:

CURITOL® (Levocarnitine) Oral Solution is for oral/internal use only.

Gastrointestinal reactions may result from too-rapid consumption of carnitine. CURITOL® (Levocarnitine) Oral Solution may be consumed alone, or dissolved in drinks or other liquid foods to reduce taste fatigue. It should be consumed slowly and doses should be spaced evenly throughout the day to maximize tolerance.

CURITOL® (Levocarnitine) Injection is for intravenous use only.

CURITOL® (Levocarnitine) Oral Solution, 330 mg Tablet and Injection:

PREGNANCY

Pregnancy Category B.

Reproductive studies have been performed in rats and rabbits at doses up to 3.8 times the human dose on the basis of surface area and have revealed no evidence of impaired fertility or harm to the fetus due to CURITOL®. There are, however, no adequate and well controlled studies in pregnant women. Because animal reproduction studies are not always predictive of human response, this drug should be used during pregnancy only if clearly needed.

NURSING MOTHERS

It is not known whether this drug is excreted in human milk. Because many drugs are excreted in human milk, a decision should be made whether to discontinue nursing or to discontinue the drug, taking into account the importance of the drug to the mother.

ADVERSE REACTIONS:

CURITOL® (Levocarnitine) Oral Solution and 330 mg Tablet:

Various mild gastrointestinal complaints have been reported during the long-term administration of oral L- or D,L-carnitine; these include transient nausea and vomiting, abdominal cramps, and diarrhea. Mild myasthenia has been described only in uremic patients receiving D,L-carnitine. Gastrointestinal adverse reactions with CURITOL® (Levocarnitine) Oral Solution dissolved in liquids might be avoided by a slow consumption of the solution or by a greater dilution. Decreasing the dosage often diminishes or eliminates drug-related patient body odor or gastrointestinal symptoms when present. Tolerance should be monitored very closely during the first week of administration, and after andy dosage increases.

CURITOL® (Levocarnitine) Injection:

Transient nausea and vomiting have been observed. Less frequent adverse reactions are body odor, nausea, and gastritis. An incidence for these reactions is difficult to estimate due to the confounding effects of the underlying pathology.

word count: 856

ASSIGNMENT 4: FINANCE

THE NEED FOR NEW APPROACHES. In the coming decade, demand for infrastructure investments will simultaneously increase in two different sets of countries: those that have undertaken macroeconomic adjustment with consequent low investment levels and, at the other extreme, those whose rapid growth is now placing a heavy burden on infrastructure. Infrastructure investments in developing countries represent, on average, 4 percent of GDP, but they often need to be substantially higher. Where telecommunications or power-supply networks are expanding rapidly, annual investments in either sector can be as high as 2 percent of GDP. A special factor increasing investment demand in many countries is the rapid pace of urbanization, requiring investments in water supply as well as waste treatment and disposal.

In Asia, the share of infrastructure investment in GDP is expected to rise from 4 percent today to more than 7 percent by the turn of the century, with transport and energy likely to demand the most resources, followed by telecommunications and environmental infrastructure. Some of the planned investments are without precedent. China, for example, has set a target of installing at least 5 million telephone lines annually up to 1995 and at least 8 million lines per year thereafter, to more than triple its 1992 base of 18 million lines by the year 2000.

Private entrepreneurship: trends and opportunities

Current efforts to secure increased private sponsorship and risktaking in infrastructure projects reflect these various challenges. After decades of severe regulatory restriction, private entrepreneurship in infrastructure bounce back in two ways during the late 1980s: through the privatization of state-owned utilities and through policy reform that made possible the construction of new facilities in competition with, or as a complement to, existing enterprises.

The principal new infrastructure entrepreneurs are international firms seeking business in developing countries and operating often in association with local companies. These firms bring to bear not only their management expertise and technical skills, but also their credit standing and ability to finance investments in developing countries. Major electric, telecommunications, and water utilities in industrial countries face slowly growing demand and increased competition (following deregulation) in their home markets. As a result, they are vigorously seeking high-yielding investments in developing countries. Construction conglomerates are active in toll-road construction and in power projects, where they sometimes take an equity interest. Some companies or groups of companies also specialize in stand-alone infrastructure projects, putting together financing packages and overseeing project development and operation.

Most indicators of infrastructure investment under private sponsorship reveal rapid growth. Privatized telecommunications and electricity utilities in Latin America and Asia are undertaking large and growing new investments. The number of these so-called greenfield projects - especially in the road and electric power sectors - has grown rapidly (as discussed below). Infrastructure investments by the International Finance Corporation (IFC), a World Bank affiliate that invests only in private entities, have experienced a surge, from modest amounts in the late 1980s to $330 million in fiscal 1993. The amount invested by the IFC was leveraged more than ten times, so that, in 1993, IFC participated in private investments of $3.5 billion.

The most important development during the past four years has been the explosion in international flows of long-term private capital to developing countries, especially in the form of foreign direct investment and portfolio flows. Aggregate flows stood at more than $80 billion in 1992 and were projected to reach $112 billion in 1993 (Table 5.1). Infrastructure has been a significant beneficiary of such flows (Box 5.2).

Aggregate private investment in infrastructure in developing countries is currently about $15 billion a year, or roughly 7 percent of the $200 billion being spent annually on infrastructure in these countries. Although small, the fraction of private investment in infrastructure investment is much larger than it was some years ago, and there is a strong likelihood that private investment will continue to grow, possibly doubling its share of the total by the year 2000. One indication is the IFC's current infrastructure pipeline, which is almost as large as all the projects financed to date.

The small overall share of private finance in infrastructure obscures large regional and sectoral disparities. Private finance is proportionately greater in Latin America than in other regions, and larger in telecommunications and electric power generation than in other sectors. The diffusion of current experience across regions and sectors will raise the global share of private sponsorship and finance. For example, telecommunications privatization and independent power generation are under discussion in all regions, including Sub-Saharan Africa. And continuing technological and financial innovations will undoubtedly make private financing more attractive. As an example, electronic methods of identifying vehicles and charging tolls could make roads more like a public utility service, and boost the share of private finance in the highway sector.

Even with the rising share of privately financed infrastructure, governments will continue to be an important source of financing. Often, they will need to be partners with private entrepreneurs. Public-private partnerships in some ways represent a return to the nineteenth century, when infrastructure projects were privately financed in much of the world while government support acted as a stimulant. But the nineteenth century experience also offers important warning signs (Box 5.3)

Table 5.1 Portfolio and foreign direct investment in developing countries, 1990–93
(net inflows in billions of dollars)

Type	*1990*	*1991*	*1992*	*1993*[a]
Foreign equity securities	3.78	7.55	13.07	13.1
Closed-end funds[b]	2.78	1.20	1.34	2.7
ADRs and GDRs[c]	0.14	4.90	5.93	7.2
Direct equity	0.77	1.45	5.80	3.2
Debt instruments	5.56	12.72	23.73	42.6
Bonds	4.68	10.19	21.24	39.1
Commercial paper	0.23	1.38	0.85	1.6
Certificates of deposit	0.65	1.15	1.64	1.8
Total portfolio[d]	9.34	20.27	36.80	55.7
Foreign direct investment	26.30	36.90	47.30	56.3
Total	35.64	57.17	84.10	112.0

Note: This table records all portfolio and direct investment flows. Separate figures for infrastructure are not available.
a. 1993 figures are estimated or projected.
b. A closed-end fund has a predetermined amount of funding and sometimes a fixed life.
c. ADR = American depositary receipts; GDR = global depositary receipts. An ADR is an instrument used by an offshore company to raise equity in the United States without formal listing on a U.S. stock exchange. GDRs are similar instruments used in Europe and elsewhere.
d. Portfolio investment is the sum of equity and debt.
Source: World Bank 1993i, pp. 10, 21.

word count: 1005

SECTION 3. TRANSLATIONS OF ASSIGNMENTS AND NOTES

ASSIGNMENT 1: TRANSLATION

Bilan d'une concession d'eau en Côte d'Ivoire

La société ivoirienne SODECI est un excellent exemple d'entreprise privée assurant un service public en Afrique de l'Ouest. Son capital, de 15 millions de dollars environs est détenu à 52 % par des intérêts nationaux, à 46 % par la Saur, société française de distribution d'eau, et à 2 % par un fonds d'investissement public. La SODECI a démarré ses activités il y a 30 ans en exploitant le réseau d'approvisionnement en eau d'Abidjan ; elle gère aujourd'hui plus de 300 réseaux d'eau courante sur l'ensemble du territoire national. Jusqu'à une époque récente, elle avait une concession pour la production d'eau à Abidjan, la capitale, et un contrat de location pour la production et la distribution d'eau dans les autres villes du pays, pour la distribution d'eau à Abidjan et pour la gestion du réseau d'assainissement de la capitale.

En raison des difficultés financières dues à la politique suivie par le gouvernement en matière de tarification et d'investissement dans le secteur au cours des années 80, le secteur de l'alimentation en eau en milieu urbain a été réorganisé. Le contrat de la SODECI pour l'approvisionnement en eau des villes a été transformé en une concession couvrant l'ensemble du pays et conférant à la SODECI la responsabilité des opérations et des investissements. Aujourd'hui, la société dessert 300.000 branchements particuliers, soit 70 % environ des 4,5 millions de citadins que compte le pays - 2 millions à Abidjan et le reste dans des agglomérations de 5.000 A 400.000 habitants. Pour permettre aux ménages à faible revenu d'avoir directement accès à l'eau, 75 % des branchements domestiques de la SODECI ont été installés gratuitement. Le nombre de branchements augmente de 5 à 6 % par an.

Depuis le début des années 70, le recouvrement intégral des coûts est de règle et les recettes provenant de la vente d'eau couvrent entièrement les dépenses d'investissement et les frais d'exploitation et d'entretien. Au cours des dix dernières années, la consommation d'eau non comptabilisée n'a jamais dépassé 15 % et le recouvrement des redevances auprès des particuliers n'a jamais été inférieur à 98 % (le recouvrement auprès des organismes publics est, en revanche, plus problématique). De surcroît, malgré la dispersion de ses opérations, la société ne compte que quatre employés pour mille branchements, ce qui la classe parmi les entreprises ayant les meilleures pratiques. Elle a aussi réussi à réduire le nombre d'expatriés dans ses effectifs, tout en développant ses opérations.

La société conserve une partie des redevances versées par les usagers pour couvrir ses dépenses -coûts d'exploitation, amortissement des actifs, extension et modernisation des réseaux de distribution - et pour verser des dividendes aux actionnaires. Elle verse par ailleurs à l'Etat un loyer, au titre du service de la dette afférente à des projets antérieurs financés par les pouvoirs publics.

La SODECI fournit un service d'une qualité proche des normes en vigueur dans les pays industriels. Son coût pour le consommateur n'en est pas pour autant plus élevé que dans les pays voisins dont la situation économique est comparable à celle de la Côte d'Ivoire, ou que dans les pays membres de la zone franc, où les tarifs couvrent rarement les coûts d'investissement, d'exploitation et d'entretien et où la qualité du service est bien inférieure. Des investisseurs privés ivoiriens détiennent maintenant la majorité du capital de la SODECI. Ses titres sont l'un des principaux produits négociés à la bourse d'Abidjan. La SODECI a distribué des dividendes à ses actionnaires et elle paie régulièrement des impôts depuis sa création.

L'approvisionnement en eau en Guinée : un exemple de contrat de location réussi

Lors de sa restructuration, en 1989, le secteur de I'approvisionnement en eau de la République de Guinée était l'un des moins développés d'Afrique de l'Ouest. A l'époque, un nouvel organisme autonome, la SONEG, a pris le contrôle du réseau urbain d'approvisionnement en eau et assumé la responsabilité de la planification et des investissements dans le secteur. La SEEG, détenue à 49 % par I'Etat et à 51 % par un consortium étranger, a été créée pour exploiter et entretenir les installations.

Aux termes du contrat de location de dix ans signé avec la SONEG, la SEEG exploite et entretient le réseau en assumant le risque commercial. Ses recettes lui viennent des redevances versées par les usagers et des droits de raccordement. La SEEG tire aussi profit des améliorations qu'elle apporte au taux de recouvrement, de la réduction des frais d'exploitation et de la diminution des quantités d'eau non comptabilisées. Etant responsable en dernier ressort des dépenses d'équipement, la SONEG est fortement incitée à fixer des tarifs appropriés et à réaliser des investissements prudents sur la base de provisions réalistes de la demande.

Pour s'assurer que les augmentations de tarif nécessaires seraient supportables par l'usager, le contrat de location prévoyait une formule inédite pour le partage des coûts. Aux termes de l'accord négocié entre le gouvernement, les deux sociétés et le pourvoyeur extérieur de fonds (la Banque mondiale), le tarif de l'eau devait être ajusté progressivement entre la première et la dixième année du contrat. Pendant cette période, la Banque mondiale acceptait de financer une part dégressive des dépenses de fonctionnement en devises, tandis que l'Etat devait, de son côté, assumer une part également dégressive du service de la dette. Au bout de la dixième année, les tarifs devaient couvrir intégralement le coût de l'eau. A ce jour, les tarifs ont augmenté plus que prévu, passant de 0,12 dollar le mètre cube en 1989 à environ 0,75 dollar en 1993. Malgré cela, le taux de recouvrement auprès des particuliers a très fortement progressé, passant de moins de 20 % à plus de 75 % en 1993 ; l'efficacité technique et la couverture du service se sont également améliorées.

Adaptation des concessions aux secteurs et aux objectifs gouvernementaux

La méthode d'attribution des concessions ou du droit d'exploitation détermine en grande partie les incitations données aux investisseurs privés. Leur permettre de réaliser des bénéfices indépendamment, ou presque, des résultats de l'entreprise revient à se priver des avantages du financement privé.

L'objectif est d'assurer aux investisseurs un taux de rentabilité financière attractif, tout en défendant l'intérêt général. Le prix payé par l'investisseur pour obtenir le droit de fournir un service - ou le niveau des subventions d'investissement ou d'exploitation susceptibles d'être accordées par l'Etat - est un élément clé de la négociation. Les autres points à négocier sont le prix de la prestation des services, la durée de la concession et les droits et obligations des parties à l'expiration du contrat.

Il s'agit d'un ensemble complexe, dont tous les éléments sont interdépendants. Immanquablement, le risque se pose que les conditions de la concession assurent à l'investisseur un taux de rentabilité trop élevé ou ne l'incitent pas suffisamment à veiller au bon entretien des équipements et à la fourniture d'un service de qualité.

Pour simplifier les choses, on a adopté certaines normes et conventions. Le plus souvent, la durée de la concession est fonction de la durée de vie de l'équipement. Ainsi, elle est généralement de 15 ans pour les centrales électriques et de 30 ans pour les routes à péage (et la plupart des centrales hydrolélectriques). Pour l'évacuation des déchets solides, la durée des contrats est de l'ordre de quatre ans, période pendant laquelle les camions poubelles se déprécient considérablement. Ceux-ci étant toutefois plus faciles à vendre que l'infrastructure des routes et des centrales électriques, les contrats peuvent ne durer que quelques mois.

Une variante intéressante est utilisée dans le secteur des télécommunications, mais elle pourrait être appliquée aussi aux centrales indépendantes. L'accent est mis non pas sur la durée de la concession, qui peut être illimitée, mais sur la durée de la période d'exclusivité. Ainsi, au Mexique et en Argentine, les entreprises nouvellement privatisées ont obtenu des licences exclusives pour une période de six à dix ans, pendant laquelle elles assument certaines obligations d'investissement. Après cela, l'Etat peut autoriser de nouvelles entreprises à s'implanter dans le secteur.

Le paiement exigé en contrepartie du droit de fournir un service peut revêtir des formes diverses. En principe, il est préférable d'attribuer la concession au soumissionnaire qui offre d'emblée la somme globale la plus importante, car un paiement initial élevé incite l'opérateur a exploiter l'installation le plus efficacement possible. Toutefois, dans le cas des grands projets, comme la route Guangzhou-Shenzhen en Chine, où les coûts et les recettes sont aléatoires, le partage des revenus ou des bénéfices permet de répartir les risques. Si l'Etat souhaite essentiellement défendre les intérêts des consommateurs, il peut renoncer à percevoir une commission et attribuer le contrat au soumissionnaire qui s'engage à fixer les tarifs les plus bas (ce qui risque ultérieurement de nuire à la qualité du service, d'où la nécessité de spécifier des normes de service minimales).

ASSIGNMENT 1: NOTES

An excellent example... (line 8) - The order of sentence is rearranged in the translation. This is a good example of how one must avoid replicating the order of words in the sentence, since each language has its own appropriate sentence structure.

SODECI (line 9) - The acronym is not expanded in the original or in the translation. Sometimes, however, you need to expand an acronym as part of the translation process, particularly when there is doubt as to whether the reader of the target language will understand the meaning of that particular acronym.

46 percent (line 10) - English text can appear as 46 percent, 46 per cent, or, more commonly, 46%. The French puts a space between 46 and %. These fine technical points are critical, and should be handled carefully, so as not to create potential misunderstandings.

concession contract (line 13) - This is translated as «concession,» probably because the English term «concession contract» does not readily translate into French, and because the meaning is not altered by this particular choice of translation.

city. It was... (line 14) - Here the translation does not follow the punctuation or the sentence pattern of the original, for obvious stylistic reasons. As long as the meaning of the original text remains intact, it is permissible to break a long, run-on sentence into shorter, more intelligible sentences or, vice-versa, combine short sentences into one cohesive sentence.

70 percent (line 21) - Notice how the word «percent» is used consistently throughout the document. As mentioned before, there are three ways in English of rendering this term, but within the body of a text it is best to select one and stick to it, to maintain clarity and consistency.
5,000 to 400,000 people (line 22) - the comma in numbers over 1000 is replaced in French by a period. The word «people» is translated as «habitants,» which conveys the same idea while being more formal.

capital and operation and maintenance costs (line 27) - Here we have somewhat technical financial terminology. While this text is too general to be considered technical, it does contain some technical terminology, as do most texts. This is important to keep in mind because a freelance translator often has to determine the degree of difficulty of a proposed translation job, whereby «technical» or «highly technical» would require more time and effort than «general.»

Lease Contract (page 2, line 5) - this is a legal term, which would usually require consulting a legal dictionary.

$0.12 (line 26) - For decimals, the French uses a comma instead of a period. In French, the dollar sign is often replaced by the spelled-out word.

Tailoring (line 29) - This is a very graphic English term using a borrowed meaning. The translator took the safe route of using the simple word «adaptation.» In non-literary translation, it is usually best to play it safe and not to look for fancy renditions.

complex brew (line 40) - Again, a graphic word, cautiously translated as «ensemble complex,» avoiding the more descriptive usage. It may have something to do with the freer spirit of American English, compared to the more traditional French usage.

ASSIGNMENT 2: TRANSLATION

ACCORD

ENTRE : NOVA INVESTMENTS, INC.

ET : SAFE MANAGEMENT LIMITED

ARTICLE I

INTRODUCTION

1.1 Date et parties à l'accord. Le présent ACCORD daté du 12 mai 1994 intervient entre Nova Investments, Inc. (LE CLIENT) une entreprise canadienne, et Safe Management Limited (SAFE), une société canadienne.

1.2 But de l'accord. Le présent ACCORD établit les termes et conditions par lesquels le Client retient les services de SAFE afin qu'elle assure la gestion et l'exploitation du Service alimentaire pour la clientèle : les employés, visiteurs et résidents du Client dans les installations (locaux) du Client situées au 1000 boulevard Étoile, Québec, H7V 3X8. Le terme «Service alimentaire» tel qu'utilisé dans le présent ACCORD, décrit le fonctionnement des installations conventionnelles, de fourniture d'alimentation, boissons et autres produits que le Client peut autoriser.

1.3 Durée de l'accord. La durée initiale du présent ACCORD est de deux (2) ans, commençant le 1er juin 1994 et renouvelable annuellement, sauf résiliation par l'une des parties dans les conditions prévues ci-dessous.

ARTICLE 4
LA DIRECTION ET LE PERSONNEL

4.1 Les employés de SAFE. SAFE devra prévoir un nombre suffisant d'employés qualifiés au niveau de la direction et du personnel pour le bon fonctionnement du Service alimentaire. Ces employés seront encadrés par le personnel de supervision et d'assistance de SAFE. Tout le personnel engagé par SAFE, devra en tout temps et pour tout, être à l'emploi exclusif de SAFE. Les accords initiaux concernant les négociations salariales et autres conditions seront les accords convenus entre les deux parties. SAFE paiera directement ses employés.

4.2 Accord sur la politique d'embauche.

a) SAFE s'engage à recruter, former, superviser, diriger, discipliner et si nécessaire, congédier du personnel travaillant au Service alimentaire.

b) Le Client ne pourra pas engager, passer des accords ou permettre
l'engagement pour ses propres services alimentaires, de personnel de direction du Service alimentaire de SAFE avant qu'un (1) an se soit écoulé après la cessation de son emploi avec SAFE ou avant un (1) an après la résiliation du présent ACCORD.

c) Le Client aura droit de regard sur le personnel de gestion.

ARTICLE 8
TERMES ET CONDITIONS GÉNÉRAUX

8.1 Taxes. SAFE percevra toutes les taxes qui s'appliquent et en remettra ces taxes aux instances concernées. Les factures d'eau et les impôts sur le chiffre d'affaires seront à la charge de SAFE.

8.2 Dispositions légales. SAFE devra se conformer aux lois, ordonnances, règles et règlements en vigueur émanant des institutions, administrations et services fédéraux, provinciaux, municipaux et locaux en charge de l'hygiène, de la sécurité et de la santé du Service alimentaire et devra se procurer et maintenir tous permis et licences nécessaires. Le Client apportera toute la coopération nécessaire à SAFE dans ses efforts à se procurer et obtenir une telle conformité.

8.3 Responsabilité d'assurance générale. SAFE doit obtenir et maintenir en vigueur au cours de la période du présent ACCORD une assurance générale contre les blessures corporelles et les dégâts matériels à concurrence d'une limite combinée d'un minimum de un million de dollars
(1 000 000.00$) incluant, mais sans s'y limiter, la responsabilité de toutes les blessures corporelles, la responsabilité contractuelle et la responsabilité contre les pertes de produits, couvrant uniquement les fonctions et les activités de SAFE prévues dans le présent ACCORD. SAFE fournira au Client les certificats correspondant aux polices d'assurance traitant de fonctionnement selon le présent ACCORD. La police d'assurance doit inclure une clause de la entreprise émettrice précisant que la police ne pourra être annulée sans qu'un préavis écrit soit donné au Client au moins trente (30) jours à l'avance.

8.4 Renonciation de recouvrement. Chacune des parties au présent ACCORD renonce reciproquement à ses droits tout comme aux droits de ses filiales et affiliés, à recouvrer de l'autre partie les pertes ou dommages aux constructions, équipements, améliorations ou autre propriété causés par le feu, une explosion ou par toute autre cause normalement incluse dans une police d'assurance standard, ou dans une assurance incendie, accidents ou responsabilité civile. Le Client gardera son bâtiment abritant le Service alimentaire, son contenu et autres propriétés assurés contre les pertes ou dommages occasionnés par le feu, une explosion et autres dégâts similaires.

ACCORD D'EXPLOITATION
entre
TELECOM-FRANCE
et
U.S.TELEPHONE

RELATIF A LA PRESTATION DE SERVICES NUMERIQUES PRIVES DE TELECOMMUNICATIONS

1. TELECOM-FRANCE et U.S.TELEPHONE acceptent par les présentes de relier des dispositifs d'exploitation afin d'offrir à la clientèle des services numériques privés via SATELLCOM WBS. Ces services seront mis en place conformément aux recommandations de C.C.I.T.T. et à la documentation appropriée de SATELLCOM WESS.

2. Tout Accord relatif à la fourniture directe d'équipements à TELECOM-FRANCE par U.S. TELEPHONE sera annexé aux présentes.

3. Aux termes du présent accord, chaque partie aura la responsabilité de fournir le segment de la liaison de communication allant des locaux du client, dans son propre pays, jusqu'au point médian de jonction de la région Atlantique ; autrement dit, pour les Etats-Unis, U.S.TELEPHONE aura la responsabilité du segment de télécommunication entre les locaux du client et le satellite ; en Côte d'Ivoire, TELECOM-FRANCE aura la responsabilité de la liaison de télécommunication entre les locaux du client et le satellite. Cependant, ces mêmes segments devront être compatibles afin de fournir les services prévus.

4. TELECOM-FRANCE et U.S. TELEPHONE devront prendre leurs propres dispositions avec leurs clients respectifs, et déterminer séparément les coûts et conditions concernant la portion des leurs services respectifs. TELECOM-FRANCE et U.S. TELEPHONE devront toutefois se communiquer leurs tarifs ainsi que toutes autres informations de commercialisation. TELECOM-FRANCE et U.S.TELEPHONE devront établir, à la demande de chaque client et pour le compte de celui-ci, des accords permettant d'établir un seul contrat et une seule facturation. Si besoin est et par accord mutuel, les parties peuvent prendre des dispositions supplémentaires. En cas d'interruption de service, il n'y aura aucune obligation financière entre TELECOM-FRANCE et U.S. TELEPHONE. Toutefois, chaque partie devra verser au client des indemnités d'interruption pour la période pendant laquelle les services ne correspondraient pas aux termes et conditions des tarifs respectifs et applicables au service en question.

5. TELECOM-FRANCE et U.S.TELEPHONE désigneront un point de contact dans leurs bureaux respectifs ; les noms de ces personnes seront communiqués pour assurer l'intégrité opérationnelle des services fournis.

6. TELECOM-FRANCE et U.S.TELEPHONE, par accord mutuel et en temps utile, pourront ajouter d'autres clauses et conditions au présent accord.

Signé pour et en   Signé pour et en

représentation de U.S.TELEPHONE	représentation de TELECOM-FRANCE
Signature :__________________	Signature :_________________
Nom :__________________	Nom :__________________
Fonction :_________________	Fonction :_________________
Date :________________	Date :_________________

ASSIGNMENT 2: NOTES

General comments:

a. Subject matter

This text represents a specific area of law, namely, business law as it applies to business agreements. With this in mind, one should be sensitive to the fact that this original English text, which relates to agreements between U.S. and Canadian and French companies repsectively, reflects Canadian and French legal terminology in this specific area. The translation is obviously intended for use in Canada and in France, and therefore should reflect local legal usage. Here a good English-French legal dictionary, as well as a basic Canadian and French legal dictionaries would be most useful.

b. Format

We draw your attention to the fact that the original text is typed in a legal text format, following established format. Therefore, the French translation was formatted to look like the original, and each page of translation corresponds exactly to each page of the original. This was done for several good reasons: (a) an end-user of a translation would often need to compare the two texts, and this exact replication makes it very easy to compare, and also to make sure nothing is missing; (b) it helps the translator to check his/her own work, making sure nothing was left out; and (c) it conveys the sense of orderliness and accuracy which is critical in legal documents.

NOVA INVESTMENT, INC. (line 8) - The name of companies remains the same in French, since it is a legal entity. Sometimes it may be necessary to provide a translation of a company's name, for information or other reasons, but the general practice is to leave the name in the original form.

AGREEMENT (line 12) - In legal documents certain words are capitalized, because of legal implications. It is important to follow this capitalization format in the text of the target language. Moreover, there are other legal terms in French for «agreement» besides *accord*, which was chosen by the present translator.

until (line 22) - The French translation reads *sauf*, which means «except.» This is a more appropriate French legal usage, which does not alter the meaning of the original.

employees (line 26) - French has both masculine and feminine forms of nouns. Therefore, you may find this word translated for both genders (employé[e]s). The translation here reflects the more traditional usage where the masculine covers both genders.

Taxes (page 2, line 15) - Here the Canadian and the European renditions may differ. Canadian French uses both *taxe* and *impôt* - both are correct. However, European usage would require *impôt*.

($1,000,000) (line 24) - Notice the omission of the commas in the French.

Points of contact (page 3, line 36) - Here the sentence structure was changed to conform to proper French syntax.

Additional observations:

Since legal documents such as business agreements contain a fairly standard text, you may want to get hold of one or more texts of such French-language agreements, to familiarize yourself with the style and terminology. Clearly, one does not always have the time and means to obtain this kind of information, but if this is a subject you expect to translate fairly regularly, it is worth the effort.

Also, it is important to know the purpose of a particular translation, although a translator is not always given this information by the client. If it is to be used as a legally binding agreement, it has to be accurate to the point of being accepted as a legal contract. On the other hand, if it is only for information purposes - say the end-user in this case does not read English - then you need not spend nearly as much time and effort to make sure every single word is the best possible equivalent of the original.

ASSIGNMENT 3: TRANSLATION

NOM DU MEDICAMENT

CURITOL®

(Lévocarnitine)

CLASSIFICATION THERAPEUTIQUE

Réapprovisionneur (Carnitine)

ACTION ET PHARMACOLOGIE CLINIQUE :

CURITOL® (Lévocarnitine) est une substance naturelle qui est nécessaire pour le métabolisme énergétique des mammifères. Il a été démontré qu'il facilite l'entrée des acides gras à longue chaîne dans la mitochondrie, delivrant un substrat pour la production d'oxydation et de l'énergie subséquente. Les acides gras sont utilisés comme un substrat d'énergie dans tous les tissus sauf dans le cerveau. Pour les muscles du coeur et du squelette ils servent de carburant principal. La première déficience en carnitine dans le système se caractérise par un bas niveau de plasma, de globules rouges, et/ou de tissus. Il n'a pas été possible de déterminer quels symptômes sont dus à une déficience en carnitine et lesquels sont dus à l'acidémie organique latente, vu que l'on s'attend à ce que les symptômes des deux anomalies s'améliorent avec la carnitine. La documentation souligne que la carnitine peut provoquer l'excrétion des excédents d'acides organiques ou gras chez les patients qui montrent des anomalies dans leur métabolisme d'acides gras et/ou des acidopathies organiques spécifiques d'accumulation biologique d'esters acyles CoA.

Une déficience secondaire de carnitine peut être une conséquence d'erreurs de métabolisme de naissance. CURITOL® pourrait diminuer les anomalies métaboliques de patients qui, à la naissance, ont des déficiences qui conduisent à une accumulation d'acides organiques toxiques. Les conditions pour lesquelles cet effet a été démontré sont: acidurie glutarique II, acidurie méthyle malonique, acidémie propionique, et une déficience de la chaîne moyenne d'acyle gras CoA déshydrogéné. Ces patients souffrent d'auto-intoxication à cause des accumulations de composés d'acyle CoA qui interrompent le métabolisme intermédiare. L'hydrolyse du composé d'acyle CoA à son acide libre qui en découle résulte en une acidose qui pourrait être fatale. Lévocarnitine élimine le composé acyle CoA en formant de l'acyle carnitine qui est rapidement excrété. Une déficience de lévocarnitine est biochimiquement définie comme ayant un niveau de plasma bas de carnitine libre, de moins de 20 µM/L à un âge supérieur à une semaine après terme et peut être associée à un bas niveau de tissus et/ou d'urine. De plus, cette condition peut être associée à une proportion de niveaux de lévocarnitine libre d'ester de plasma supérieure à 0,4 ou à des niveaux anormalement élevés de lévocarnitine estérifiée dans l'urine. Chez les nourrissons et prématurés, une déficience secondaire est définie comme de bas niveaux de levocarnitine sans plasma au-dessous des niveaux normaux correspondants à l'âge.

INDICATIONS ET UTILISATION CLINIQUE:

CURITOL® (lévocarnitine) solution par voie orale (1 g/10 Ml Multidose), comprimé de 330 mg et par injection (1 g par 5 ml);

CURITOL® (lévocarnitine) est indiqué premièrement pour le traîtement des déficiences de carnitine dans le système. Dans les cas documentés, la présentation clinique consistait en épisodes répétés d'encéphalopathie ressemblant à la maladie de Reye, hypoglycémie hypokétotique, et/ou cardiomyopathie. Les symptômes qui y étaient associés comprenaient de l'hypotonie, faiblesse des muscles et manque de développement. Un diagnostique de déficience majeure de carnitine demande que les niveaux de carnitine du sérum, des globules rouges et/ou des tissus soient bas et que le patient n'ait pas un défaut important d'oxydation d'acides gras ou organiques (voir la Pharmacologie clinique). Chez quelques patients, particulièrement ceux qui présentent une cardiomyopathie, un supplément de carnitine a rapidement soulagé leurs symptômes. Le traîtement doit inclure, en plus de la carnitine, une thérapie de soutien et autre, selon la condition du patient.

CURITOL® (lévocarnitine) est aussi indiqué pour le traitement grave et chronique de patients qui souffrent d'une erreur de métabolisme de naissance qui résulte en une déficience secondaire de carnitine.

CONTRE INDICATIONS :

Aucune connue.

AVERTISSEMENTS :

Aucun.

PRECAUTIONS :

GENERALITÉS:

CURITOL® (lévocarnitine) solution par voie orale :

CURITOL® (lévocarnitine) solution par voie orale doit être administré par voie orale/interne uniquement.

Des réactions gastro-intestinales peuvent survenir, causées par la consommation rapide de la carnitine. CURITOL® (lévocarnitine) solution par voie orale peut être avalé seul ou mélangé dans une boisson ou autre aliment liquide pour éviter de se lasser du goût. Il doit être bu lentement, et les doses doivent être espacées à intervalles réguliers pendant la journée pour une plus grande tolérance.

CURITOL® (lévocarnitine) par injection s'utilise par voie intraveineuse uniquement.

CURITOL® (lévocarnitine) solution par voie orale, comprimé de 330 mg et par injection:

GROSSESSE :

Grossesse catégorie B.

Des études sur la reproduction ont été faites sur des rats et des lapins à doses 3,8 fois la dose pour humains, basées sur l'étendue de la surface, et elles n'ont révélé aucune évidence de réduction de fertilité ni de dommage au fétus attribuable à CURITOL®. Cependant, il n'y a pas d'études adéquates ni bien contrôlées quant aux femmes enceintes. Les études sur la reproduction des animaux ne reflétant pas toujours la réaction chez les humains, ce médicament ne devrait être administré aux femmes enceintes que lorsqu'il est absolument nécessaire.

MERES QUI ALLAITENT :

Il n'est pas démontré que ce médicament soit excrété dans le lait humain. Du fait que beaucoup de médicaments sont excrétés dans le lait humain, il faudrait prendre la décision de cesser l'allaitement ou d'arrêter le traîtement avec ce médicament, selon l'importance du rôle que joue le médicament pour la mère.

REACTIONS ADVERSES :

CURITOL® (lévocarnitine) solution par voie orale et comprimé de 330 mg :

Plusieurs légères affections intestinales ont été signalées au cours d'une administration prolongée de carnitine L- ou D,L- par voie orale ; elles comprennent des périodes de nausées et de vomissements, des douleurs abdominales et des diarrhées. De légères myasthénies se sont manifestées, mais seulement chez les patients souffrant d'urémie qui prenaient de la carnitine
D,L-. En prenant le CURITOL® (lévocarnitine) solution par voie orale mélangé dans du liquide, les réactions gastro-intestinales adverses peuvent être évitées en buvant la solution lentement ou en la mélangeant dans une plus grande quantité de liquide. Une diminution de la dose peut souvent atténuer ou même éliminer l'odeur corporelle du patient causée par le médicament ainsi que les symptômes gastro-intestinaux qui pourraient exister. La tolérance au médicament devrait être contrôlée pendant la première semaine d'administration, ainsi qu'après une augmentation de la dose.

CURITOL® (lévocarnitine) par injection :

Des périodes de nausées et vomissements ont été observées. De fréquentes réactions adverses sont l'odeur corporelle, la nausée et la gastrite. Il est difficile d'estimer l'incidence de ces réactions à cause des effets de la pathologie sous-jacente qui prête à confusion.

ASSIGNMENT 3: NOTES

General comments:

a. Subject matter

Though this particular assignment presents many examples of specific terminology, the text itself is straightforward, and presents no real difficulty in terms of sentence structure or language style. Unless one is thoroughly familiar with the chemical and pharmacological terms in this text, it would be best not to start translating right away, but first to make a list of all such terms in the text one is not certain of.

b. References

A good chemical/pharmacological dictionary should have all or nearly all the technical terms of this text. If after thorough consultation with such a source you still have an unknown term, the next thing to do is call someone with an appropriate professional background.

Bear in mind that exact sciences such as chemistry and pharmacology have a well-defined and fairly limited vocabulary. After doing this kind of an assignment several times you will be able to do it much faster and with minimal time spent on research.

CURITOL® (line 8) - The technical symbol ® used in this context is typical of technical and science symbols frequently used in this kind of translation. Here computer software is a must, along with a chart of such symbols, which is provided with all the major word processing programs.

RBC (line 17) - This is a familiar scientific acronym, readily translatable into French. This may not always be the case with acronyms in texts of this kind. Good acronym dictionaries, glossaries or self-generated lists are critical for the translator of this kind of material.

0.4: (line 33) - in French the decimal point becomes a comma.

Oral Solution is for oral/internal use only (page 2, line 26) - Here the translation adds certain explanatory words to make the meaning more clear. Sometimes this approach, though not to be encouraged, is unavoidable.

ASSIGNMENT 4: TRANSLATION

DES APPROCHES NOUVELLES S'IMPOSENT. Dans les dix prochaines années, la demande d'investissements d'infrastructure augmentera simultanément dans deux groupes de pays : ceux qui ont entrepris un ajustement macroéconomique qui freine les investissements et, à l'autre extrémité, ceux dont la croissance rapide soumet l'infrastructure à une forte pression. Les investissements d'infrastructure dans les pays en développement représentent, en moyenne, 4 % du PIB, mais les besoins sont souvent substantiellement plus grands. Lorsque les télécommunications ou les réseaux de transport de l'électricité se développent rapidement, les investissements annuels dans chacun de ces secteurs peuvent atteindre 2 % du PIB. En outre, la demande d'investissement augmente dans beaucoup e pays sous l'influence d'une urbanisation rapide qui oblige à investir dans l'approvisionnement en eau et le traitement et l'élimination des déchets.

En Asie, la part des investissements d'infrastructure dans le PIB devrait passer d'un pourcentage actuel de 4 % à plus de 7 % d'ici la fin du siècle, les transports et l'énergie venant probablement au premier rang, suivis par les télécommunications et l'infrastructure environnementale. Certains investissements prévus sont sans précédent. La Chine, par exemple, s'est fixé pour objectif d'installer au moins 5 millions de lignes téléphoniques chaque année jusqu'en 1995, et au moins 8 millions de lignes par an ultérieurement, afin que, d'ici l'an 2000, elle ait plus que triplé les 18 millions de lignes en place en 1992.

Initiative privée : tendances et possibilités

Les efforts faits actuellement pour inciter les entrepreneurs privés à prendre la responsabilité des projets d'infrastructure et à en assumer les risques sont la conséquence directe de la situation décrite plus haut. Après plusieurs décennies de réglementations très restrictives, l'initiative privée a, à la fin des années 80, réaffirmé de deux manières sa place dans le secteur de l'infrastructure : dans le cadre de la privatisation des entreprises de services publics appartenant à l'Etat, ainsi que du changement de politique que a permis la construction d'installations nouvelles concurrençant ou complétant les entreprises existantes.

Les entrepreneurs qui font leur apparition dans le domaine de l'infrastructure sont principalement des sociétés internationales qui cherchent à s'implanter dans les pays en développement et qui opèrent souvent en association avec des entreprises locales. Elles apportent avec elles non seulement leurs compétences de gestion et leur savoir technique, mais aussi la qualité de leur crédit et les moyens dont elles disposent pour financer des investissements dan ces pays. Dans les secteurs de l'électricité, des télécommunications et des eaux, les grandes entreprises de services publics des pays industriels se heurtent, chez elles, à une demande ralentie et à une concurrence de plus en plus vive (à la suite de la déréglementation). Aussi recherchent-elles activement des investissements à haut rendement dans les pays en développement. On voit ainsi des conglomérats d'entreprises de construction exécuter des chantiers de construction de routes à péage ainsi que des projets d'équipement électrique dans lesquels ils prennent parfois un intérêt participatif. On en trouve aussi qui se spécialisent dans la réalisation de projets d'infrastructure autonomes, assurant les montages financiers et supervisant la mise au point et le fonctionnement des opérations.

La plupart des indicateurs des investissements d'infrastructure sous contrôle privé dénotent une croissance rapide. Les sociétés de services publics privatisées dans les secteurs des télécommunications et de l'électricité, augmente rapidement (comme on l'expose ci-après). Les investissements d'infrastructure de la Société financière international (SFI), membre du Groupe de la Banque mondiale qui investit uniquement dans les entreprises privées, ont littéralement bondi, passant de sommes modestes à la fin des années 80 à 330 millions de dollars pour l'exercice 93. Comme le montant investi par la SFI a permis de mobiliser des financements plus de dix fois supérieurs, la Société a donc participé à 3,5 milliards de dollars d'investissements en 1993.

Les quatre dernières années ont été marquées principalement par le gonflement considérable des flux internationaux de capitaux privés à long terme vers les pays en développement, surtout sous la forme d'investissements étrangers directs et de flux de portefeuille. Ces flux, qui dépassaient les 80 milliards de dollars en 1992, devaient s'élever à 112 milliard de dollars en 1993, selon les prévisions (Tableau 5.1). L'infrastructure a bénéficié notablement de cette évolution (Encadré 5.2).

Le montant total des investissements privés d'infrastructure dans les pays en développement s'élève actuellement à près de 15 milliards de dollars par an,soit environ 7 % des 200 milliards de dollars dépensés annuellement pour l'infrastructure dans ces pays. Quoique modeste, la proportion des investissements privés dans les investissements d'infrastructure est beaucoup plus forte qu'il y a quelques années, et tout porte à croire que l'investissement privé continuera d'augmenter, allant peut-être jusqu'à doubler sa part du total d'ici l'an 2000. Ainsi, les projets d'infrastructure actuellement en cours de préparation à la SFI portent sur un montant presque aussi élevé que celui de tous les projets financés jusqu'à présent.

La modeste part globale du financement privé dans l'infrastructure masque d'importantes disparités régionales et sectorielles. Le financement privé est proportionnellement plus élevé en Amérique latine que dans les autres régions, et plus important dans les télécommunications et dans la production d'électricité que dans les autres secteurs. La diffusion des leçons de l'expérience actuelle dans les différentes régions et les divers secteurs fera augmenter la proportion globale des projets dirigés et financés par des entreprises privées. Ainsi, la privatisation des télécommunications et l'ouverture de la production d'électricité aux entrepreneurs indépendants sont à-l'étude dans toutes les régions, y compris l'Afrique subsaharienne. Et il ne fait pas de doute que le cours ininterrompu de l'innovation technique et financière rendra le financement privé plus attrayant. Par exemple, les méthodes électroniques d'identification des véhicules et de perception des péages pourraient rendre les routes plus assimilables à un service d'utilité publique et accroître la part des financements privés dans le secteur routier.

Même avec la multiplication des services d'infrastructure financés par les capitaux privés, l'Etat demeurera une importante source de financement des équipements collectifs. Il lui faudra souvent intervenir en partenariat avec les entrepreneurs privés. D'une certaine manière, l'association entre pouvoirs publics et intérêts privés marque un retour à la situation du XIXe siècle, contient aussi d'importants enseignements à méditer (Encadré 5.3).

Tableau 5.1 Investissements de portefeuille et investissements étrangers directs vers les pays en développement, 1990-93

(entrées nettes en milliards de dollars)

Type	*1990*	*1991*	*1992*	*1993*[a]
Investissements étrangers de participation	3,78	7,55	13,07	13,1
Sociétés d'investissement à capital fixe[b]	2,78	1,20	1,34	2,7
ADR et GDR[c]	0,14	4,90	5,93	7,2
Participations directes	0,77	1,45	5,80	3,2
Instruments d'endettement	5,56	12,72	23,73	42,6
Obligations	4,68	10,19	21,24	39,1
Effets de commerce	0,23	1,38	0,85	1,6
Certificats de dépôt	0,65	1,15	1,64	1,8
Total portefeuille[d]	9,34	20,27	36,80	55,7
Investissements étrangers directs	26,30	36,90	47,30	56,3
Total	35,64	57,17	84,10	112,0

Note : Ce tableau porte sur la totalité des flux de portefeuille et d'investissement direct. On ne dispose pas de chiffres séparés pour l'infrastructure.

a. Les chiffres pour 1993 proviennent d'estimations ou de projections.

b. Une société d'investissement à capital fixe a un capital d'un montant déterminé d'avance et peut avoir une durée d'existence fixe.

c. ADR = American Depository Receipts (reçus de dépôts américains); GDR = Global Depository Receipts (reçus de dépôts mondiaux). Un ADR permet à une société extraterritoriale de se procurer des fonds aux États-Unis sans être inscrite officiellement à la cote d'une bourse des valeurs américaine. Les GDR sont des instruments similaires utilisés en Europe et ailleurs.

d. L'investissement de portefeuille est égal à la somme des participations et de l'endettement.

Source : Banque mondiale, 1993h, p. 10, 21.

ASSIGNMENT 4: NOTES

General comments:

a. Financial Translation

In translation, there is a basic difference between translating financial subjects and other technical subjects, such as legal or medical. While it is relatively easy to master the methodology of working with most technical vocabularies, even if one does not have the technical or professional background of the particular field in which one translates, in financial subjects it is necessary to have at least a general knowledge of the subject. This may be due to the fact that financial terminology and concepts are not always as readily translatable as other technical subjects. The upshot of all this is that one should not be hasty to accept a financial translation assignment if one does not work in this field on a regular basis.

b. Subject matter

This particular assignment consists of a text derived from a publication of an international financial organization. As with most major organizations and corporations, this organization has its own so-called «corporate style,» which affects the way this material is translated. Normally, an organization of this magnitude employs its own translators, or uses outside translators on a regular basis, to acquaint them with its style. If called upon to translate this kind of text, be sure to familiarize yourself with the organization's style.

THE NEED FOR NEW APPROACHES (line 8) - Here the French rendition deviates somewhat from the meaning of the original. Instead of «the need,» we have *s'imposent*, «imposing themselves.» This approach can be questioned, but in this context it does not seem to cause any real problem to the essence of this opening paragraph.

GDP (line 12) - This is a familiar acronym in the field of economics, and has its French equivalent. Other acronyms won't be so readily translatable, and one can either find a good reference to look them up or check with the client.

7 percent (line 18) - Whether you use the word or the symbol for percentage, be consistent and use the same item throughout.

The principal new infrastructure... (line 29) - Here the sentence structure is changed in translation to better accommodate French syntax. The paragraph in general is an example of some slight rewriting or rephrasing which is typical in financial and economic writing, where one frequently needs more than just a simple replication to convey ideas and ensure their cohesiveness and logical sequence.

International Finance Corporation (IFC) (line 43) - Here the name of the organization is translated into French, and the IFC becomes the SFI. This is an example of an acronym which may not be universally familiar.

$330 million (page 2, line 5) - In French the U.S. currency is spelled out rather than indicated by its symbol, a common French usage.

$3.5 billion (line 7) - The period becomes comma in French.

Additional notes:

The table at the end of this assignment consists of technical financial language. Here thorough familiarity with this kind of terminology, and with the institution that generates such terminology is critical. In undertaking this kind of translation, one should have a good line of communication with the organization that generates this text, to be sure the client and the translator are on the same wavelength.

SECTION 4

WHERE DO I GO FROM HERE?

After you have completed all the assignments, or at least those you have chosen to do, you have to make a major decision. If you have never translated for profit before, you have to ask yourself if you are ready to try your hand at soliciting for-profit translation work. If the answer is yes, turn to the book in this Kit, *Guide for Translators,* and read Chapters 9 and 10, on how to operate successfully as a freelance translator, and where to find work. If you have translated for profit before in a specific area, such as legal documents, and you feel you are now ready to venture into another area, such as medical translation, first try out some short assignments in that field, until you become comfortable with it.

In either case, the next step is to turn to Appendix 3 in the book, and look up sources of translation work. We urge you to develop a relationship with one or more translation companies in your own geographical area. There is absolutely no reason in this day and age for a translator, say, in Wisconsin, not to develop a profitable relationship with a translation company in Florida, and in time you may indeed find out that a certain company on the other side of the continent is your best source of work. But as a beginner, there are many advantages to interfacing personally with the staff of a translation company close to home. They can give you a great deal of practical advice, help you with the hardware and the software, and share other kinds of experience with you. There is an old saying: A good neighbor is better than a distant relative.

If, on the other hand, you feel you are not ready to take the plunge, you may want to consider a translation course or study program. Refer to Appendix 4 in the book, and see if there is a program close to home you can sign up for. Or you may decide to continue practicing on your own.

Whatever you decide to do, don't give up too easily. If you do enjoy the challenge of translation, continue to improve you skills. Remember: Translation can be a full-time career or a very fulfilling and profitable sideline. It is definitely the kind of expertise worth having, no matter what else you choose to do with your time.

Translator Self-Training Program

French-into-English Workbook

Schreiber Publishing

Rockville, Maryland

Table of Contents

SECTION 1. GENERAL

INTRODUCTION

Welcome to *Schreiber's* **Translator Self-Training Program**. We are very pleased you selected this program, which has been in use since 1992. It has helped aspiring translators around the country get their start in this exciting field, while assisting practicing translators in improving their translation skills. Translation is one of the fastest growing professions in today's world, as different languages and cultures are coming closer together every day. Whether you wish to pursue translation full-time or as a sideline, you will find it to be a highly challenging and quite profitable occupation. The purpose of the following exercises is to help you improve your skills as a French-into-English translator.

This program is designed to help you work at your own pace and gain experience through translation practice assignments. These assignments, excerpted from actual translation jobs, were selected to help you determine your own level of comfort and expertise, so that you may go on from there to choose the type of translation work you might like to pursue.

To derive the maximum benefit from these texts, you should carefully read the General Comments, the guidelines, and the specific notes which discuss each assignment. Every comment and every guideline represents years of experience in professional translation work. By carefully following this program, you will be able to achieve *in just a few days* what has taken others years to learn. You will be guided through many of the pitfalls of translation, taught how to avoid them, shown shortcuts in accomplishing a complex piece of translation work, and be given the benefit of comments designed to show you how to produce a translation acceptable to major clients such as government, industry, the legal world, and many more.

Before you read further, we strongly urge you to read the following chapters in the book *Guide for Translators,* included in this kit:

Chapter 3: Basic Requisites for Becoming a Professional Translator
Chapter 4: The Well-Rounded Translator
Chapter 5: Good and Bad Translation Habits
Chapter 6: Translation Techniques
Chapter 7: Translation Equipment
Chapter 8: Dictionaries and Reference Literature

The above-listed chapters will give you a good overview of how translation work is to be approached and practiced. Try to keep the contents of these chapters in mind as you translate the following assignments.

You are presented with four different texts, which, for most people, represent an increasing level of difficulty (although if you happen to be a lawyer, for example, it is possible that you will find the second assignment the easiest of the four). They are:

1. **General**
2. **Legal**

3. **Chemical/Medical**
4. **Business/Finance**

At a minimum, you may want to do the first and second assignments. Those two represent a vast body of material which is being translated in the United States on a regular basis, but which does not require a highly specialized vocabulary or technical background. The third assignment requires access to chemical and medical terminology, which can be managed by any intelligent translator. The fourth assignment should be approached with caution. Here one must have an understanding of the world of finance, which not all of us do. For your own self-assessment, you may want to try it (since we provide you with the translation, you can compare the results and see for yourself how you did). But if you find it too difficult, don't be discouraged. It is clearly not for everyone.

We hope you enjoy working with these texts, and we urge you to please be patient with yourself. One does not become an accomplished translator overnight. To learn, one must make mistakes. If your heart is in it, and if you love the challenge of working with two languages you happen to know well, then you are sure to get a great deal out of this program.

A Word about French Translation

French, once the language of international diplomacy and the favorite of cultivated people everywhere, is still today one of the world's major languages in nearly every field of human endeavor. It is one of the leading languages in both Europe and Africa, the second language of Canada, the language of Caribbean nations like Haiti, and it is widely studied in many countries around the world.

Many American college students choose French for their foreign language requirement, or even major in this language. From all indications, given the popularity of the French language and the continued economic and cultural importance of France, French should continue to play a significant role on the international scene in the next century.

This means that developing one's skills as a French-into-English or English-into-French translator is time well spent. The United States and France continue to interact in all areas of commerce, science and technology. Documentation and literature flow between the two countries and between the U.S. and other French speaking parts of the world in a steady stream and in both directions. As the global village becomes more of a reality with every passing day, the interaction between French and English intensifies, and requires an ever-growing volume of translation in real time.

Some maintain that in time English will replace other languages such as French, Spanish, German, etc. and will become the one language used by everyone in all international activities. Such claims were made in the past - in the time of the Roman Empire, for example. The fact remains, however, that at any given time in history there were always multiple cultural centers in the world, and even here in the United States, where English has been the dominant language for at least two centuries, other languages are gaining importance, and cultural pluralism, rather than disappearing, is flourishing.

The following exercises are designed to help you achieve a worthy and profitable goal - becoming an expert in improving communications between two of the world's major cultures and tongues - English and French.

GENERAL COMMENTS

The following comments are offered with two purposes in mind: the immediate purpose is to help you with the assignments. The long-term purpose is to serve as reference material for actual translation work. Keep them for future use.

A reminder:
The "source language" is the language you translate from.
The "target language" is the language you translate into.

Every language has its own "personality," so to speak. When you translate, pretend you are two different persons - an "English Person" and a "French Person." The French Person reads the original French text, and becomes familiar with it. The French Person then turns to the English Person, and says to him/her, "**Okay, now it's your turn to say the same thing your way**.» Now the English Person takes over, and starts writing the same text in English. You will be constantly switching back and forth between the French Person and the English Person, as the first checks the French word, phrase, sentence structure, and then the second thinks in English and comes up with the right equivalents. Here are some of the main language issues you will have to deal with:

Clarity

We each have our own personal style of expressing ourselves - in any language. Some people make their point clearly and succinctly, while others use more words than necessary, including esoteric words, to make their point. The same holds true in translation. You can translate the phrase, «chacun à son goût,» as «it's a matter of taste,» or you could also translate it correctly as, «each person has his or her own different taste.» In the first instance, only five words were used; in the second, nine. Most of the time, the first type of translation is better, because it is simpler and more readily understandable. Make it your point to pursue simplicity whenever possible.

Consistency

Most of the time, if you start out translating the word «maison» as «house,» stick to «house,» and don't start suddenly shifting to «building,» or vice versa. The reader may become confused, wondering why the word suddenly changed. Generally in English, building is bigger than house, and one may wonder whether the dimensions of that particular structure might have changed. If you are familiar with word-processing you know how easy it is to do a «global search and replace» throughout the text, so that if halfway into the document you decide that «building» is better than «house,» then go back to the beginning and do a global change, replacing the word «house» with «building.»

Sentence Structure

It is difficult, yet very important, to ensure that sentence structure is correct and makes sense, yet still retains the flavor of the original text, particularly if this is written in a flowery, elaborate, or otherwise unique style. This fine line is achieved mainly through practice, but it is definitely helpful to read the original several times before even beginning the translation process in order to gain a good idea of the author's style.

It is not necessary to follow the structure of a sentence literally. A run-on sentence which may make sense in one language may not make sense in the other, and therefore should be divided into two sentences (or more). The converse is also true. You should also avoid being too literal when it comes to word order or your text will sound stilted, awkward, and artificial. You will need to rely on your own good writing skills in determining the most sensible word order and punctuation so that your translation flows smoothly.

Format

Format should be followed as closely as possible. Ideally, every page of translation should look exactly like the corresponding page of the original, except, of course, for the language. There is a very practical reason for this. It helps the reader, who may or may not know the source language, compare the two texts, make sure all the parts are there, and check a particular word or phrase in the source text. This, however, is not always possible, since a page of translation at times is longer than the same page in the source language. Nevertheless, every effort should be made to keep the format as similar as possible to the original.

Terminology

The use of the right terminology is critical in any translation, especially in any technical subject. Here the right kind of dictionaries and reference literature becomes very critical. Keep in mind, however, that dictionaries, no matter how good, are never complete, and do not provide all the answers. The other source of information is people who work in the field the particular translation covers. Their input is often more valuable than that of the dictionary, since they are the ones who work in the field and represent the potential readers of your translation.

The first thing to keep in mind about terminology - as was discussed before - is consistency. If you translate a word a certain way, do not change in the middle of the text to another synonym of the same word, even though it may be accurate. This will throw the reader off. The second thing is to make sure you are using the right terms, rather than trying to approximate them. Keep a list of those terms to maintain consistency throughout the document, and also for future use. If you continue to translate in the same technical field, these lists will become your most valuable translation tool.

Numbers

The use of commas and periods is reversed in numbers over 1000 (1.000 in French becomes 1,000 in English), and in decimals (0,5 in French, becomes 0.5 in English). This is one example of cultural differences which must be closely observed.

Punctuation

Quotation marks are appropriate in English, but this is not always so in French. Semicolons have their place in both languages, but not necessarily in the same places. These are just a few examples of how even a highly accurate translation will not always mirror its original text. You will often be called upon to be the judge, which involves a combination of excellent writing skills, knowledge of rules of grammar and punctuation, plus common sense.

Errors in the Source Text

Sometimes you will find that the original has errors, such as a misspelling where it is clear by the context that the author intended to say «une» and not «un,» or the sequence in a series of numbered clauses is wrong, or a name that has been in upper case letters suddenly appears as lower case, for no apparent reason. You can do a number of things in situations such as these. You can go ahead and make the correction and leave it at that. You can translate the text as is, and use the term [sic] after the error, to alert the reader. Or you can make a translator's note on a separate sheet of paper. Ultimately, the client will have to decide what to do with it.

Untranslatable Words or Terms

You may run into a word, a term or a phrase which cannot be translated, or which should be left in the original language (such as, for instance, vichyssoise). If there is a need to explain it, it can be done in a footnote or in parentheses (or brackets, which makes it clearer that the bracketed text is not part of the original) following the word (vichyssoise [potato, leek and cream soup, served cold]). As a general rule, however, it is best not to burden your translation with footnotes or parenthetic or bracketed text.

In Conclusion

The above notes are by no means exhaustive. They do not cover all the issues facing a translator. Language is not mathematics. Keep this in mind, and do the best translation job you possibly can.

GUIDELINES FOR TRANSLATING THE ASSIGNMENTS

1. We are providing you with a French text and an English translation of that same text. Pretend you don't have the English translation. If you read it before you do the assignment, you will not be able to do an honest job, and you will not derive the benefit of learning from your own mistakes.

2. Read the French text once for general comprehension. Underline any difficult words or passages.

3. As you start the translation process by reading the text for the first time (see 2., above), keep track of time, so that when you finish you will know how long it took you to translate the text. This is very critical, because you want to increase your translation speed as you go along. The rule is simple: the more words you translate per hour, the more money you will make. A very low hourly word-count can earn you less than minimum wage, which is not at all desirable. (Note: The hours indicated at the top right hand corner for each assignment include two numbers. The first is for beginners while the second number is for an experienced translator. Therefore, an assignment that would take a beginner 5-7 hours to complete might take an experienced translator 2 hours. The timeframe includes research, draft, and final copy.)

4. Read it again. This time make a list of difficult words, and make any notes regarding things you need to clarify about the text (e.g., look up something in an encyclopedia to better understand some concept or piece of information).

5. Try to determine which dictionaries and reference books you need for this assignment, get a hold of them, and keep them nearby.

6. Now you are ready to start translating. Preferably, you will be using a computer. If this is too intimidating, write it out the first time. It will take longer, but you will have more time to think. Remember, your objective is to translate on computer, not in longhand. These days, if you want to earn money translating, you have to submit text on disk. There are hardly any exceptions to this requirement.

7. Do a draft translation. Go over the draft. Do the best you can to make the English sound like good, clear, correct English which does not sound like French and does not retain any French forms in either style, format, or any technical points. Be sure you did not omit anything. Ask yourself if you succeeded in conveying the correct sense of every idea and every word in the source text. Be sure you are comfortable with every single word you chose in English, and that you have no doubts or hesitations. If, after all this, you do have some questions, do not worry. No one expects you to do perfect work the first time around. You will do better next time.

8. Now that you have accomplished your translation, figure out the time it took you to reach your final version (including all the previous steps - namely, first reading, research, draft, and final copy).

9. Make a list of the words, passages, and concepts in the text where you encountered difficulty, and keep for future reference. This kind of record keeping will help you improve your performance, and serve as a reminder not to repeat the same mistake twice.

10. Print out your corrected and edited text.

GUIDELINES FOR SELF-EVALUATION

1. Turn to the English translation in Section 3, and compare it to yours. Next read the notes concerning the pitfalls and salient points of this text very carefully, and see how they compare to your own experience with the text. They may not necessarily coincide with everything you experienced personally, but they do provide you with some tips on the do's and don'ts of technical translation

2. The most important thing for you to keep in mind as you compare your translation to the one in Section 3, is that there is no one absolutely correct way of translating a text. Many words can be translated in more than one way. Many sentences can be structured in more than one way. Many ideas can be conveyed in different words. In fact, your translation may turn out to be just as good, and in some spots even better than the one in the book.

3. Keep track of the shortcomings of your translation. The areas you are interested in are the following:

   Omissions - did you fail to translate any particular word or phrase, or even paragraph?

   Format - does your format follow the original (breaking into paragraphs, for instance)?

   Mistranslations - did you mistranslate any particular word?

   Unknown words - were there any words you were not able to translate?

   Meaning - did you miss the meaning of any particular phrase or sentence?

   Spelling - did you misspell a word?

   Grammar - did you make any grammatical mistakes?

   Punctuation - did you mispunctuate or miss any punctuation marks?

   Clarity - did you fail to clearly convey the meaning of any particular part of the text?

   Consistency - did you call something by one name, and then by another without good reason?

   Cognates - were you «tripped» by a word in the source text, whereby you mistranslated it because it looked the same, though it changes meaning in the target language (for instance, the word «actual»[«actuel»] exists in both English and French, but means two different things)?

Style - are you satisfied with the way your translation reflects the style of the original (for example, the original is written in a clear, direct style, while the translation sounds more complex and indirect)?

These are some of the questions you have to ask yourself. As you go on to translate other texts, always keep these questions in mind as you self-assess your translation. By improving your performance in the above areas, you are on your way to becoming an accomplished translator.

SECTION 2. ASSIGNMENTS

3.5-4.5/1.5 hours

ASSIGNMENT 1 : GENERAL

Que dire du dace, que les ancêtres des Roumains parlaient avant que les troupes de Trajan les soumettent ? Et du pannonien, parlé dans la plaine du Danube ? Et de l'étrusque, pour la région de Florence ? Et de l'ibère ? Et du carthaginois ? Et du ligure ? Que dire de toutes ces langues ? Rien. Elles sont mortes. Disparues. Ce sont des énigmes, des mystères. Il en va de même du gaulois. Contrairement à ce que croient les francophones mal informés, le nombre de mots dont l'étymologie gauloise est avérée en français - sur un ensemble que l'on peut évaluer à 40 000 mots - ne dépasse pas la centaine ! L'historien, médiéviste ou autre, dispose de manuscrits ; le géologue, lui, peut interroger la roche ; le physicien, les gaz. Mais le linguiste professionnel qui s'aventure dans la diachronie - dans le temps - n'a guère l'espérance d'avoir un matériau manipulable, feuille ou parchemin. Son unique recours, c'est la mémoire. La transmission orale. Il y a des transmissions orales que traversent des siècles et des siècles. D'autres, pas. Devant ce constat d'exhumation impossible d'un certain passé - et donc, du savoir - je ne perds pas le sommeil. Je ne suis ni morose ni pessimiste. Mais il convient d'en tirer une philosophie du présent et de l'avenir.

Vous avez dû déjà l'entendre, mais je vous le ressers quand même : l'expérience prouve que moins on en sait plus on croit qu'on en sait ; et que plus on en sait plus on sait combien on ne sait pas. Ce principe s'applique à merveille au linguiste de terrain, à l'enquêter. Pour une raison très simple, numérique et chiffrée : le monde contemporain compte environ de 7 000 à 7 500 langues. Celles pour lesquelles nous disposons de descriptions, de monographies sous forme de grammaire et de vocabulaire ne constituent pas la moitié. Et, en plus, pour la plupart, ces langues de tradition orale sont en voie d'extinction. Que ce soit en Afrique - mon domaine de prédilection - ou en Nouvelle-Guinée, si le linguiste ne se précipite pas avec son magnétophone pour enregistrer les derniers phonèmes balbutiés par des vieillards malades qui, déjà, ne parlent plus très bien leur langue car ils ne la pratiquent qu'entre eux - et sans jamais l'avoir transmise aux jeunes - alors, il n'y aura demain plus aucune trace de la langue en question. Il y a donc un phénomène d'urgence. Une motivation à ne pas aggraver le déficit de la connaissance. Nous nous livrons à des descriptions synchroniques - horizontales - des structures actuelles de la langue. Notre matériau est vivant : c'est l'être humain. Mais quand notre informateur ne sait pas - ou ne sait plus - on ne peut pas inventer à sa place.

Une seule fois, en 1976, dans une ethnie africaine du centre du Cameroun, j'ai eu la joie d'assister à la naissance d'un mot. En découvrant mon magnétophone, mon informateur a créé dans sa langue - le mbum - le mot "calebasse à paroles". L'année suivante, quand je suis revenu, le mot était consacré et on ne se rappelait plus qui l'avait inventé. L'oubli de la paternité d'un mot est à considérer comme un critère de son succès. J'ajoute que si la linguistique et une science, l'étymologie n'en est pas une. C'est une pratique. Neuf fois sur dix, nous ne savons pas vraiment d'où vient un mot.

Dans le contexte d'urgence, vous en conviendrez, vouloir reconstituer le passé est un luxe. Fondée sur le comparatisme, à partir des langues attestées aujourd'hui et en observant des racines communes, la linguistique est quand même parvenue - avec un part de présomption - à reconstituer des bases très anciennes, unifiées, de bon nombre de nos langues. Mais au-delà des langues ancêtres, des familles de langues - l'indo-européen, l'altaïque, le sino-tibétain, etc. - il y a des mystères. D'où vient le basque ? Et d'où viennent les Basques ? Ils furent probablement les premiers habitants de l'Europe, mais leur langue n'est rattachée à rien, à aucune famille. Le basque, c'est quoi ? Eh bien, le basque, c'est le basque : une des plus belles énigmes de la linguistique.

La linguistique se veut une science humaine et ne relève pas du domaine de la recherche poétique. Ce qui ne veut pas dire que tous ces grands points d'interrogation, que tous ces aspects magiques, lyriques et romanesques ne jouent pas un rôle majeur en tant que motivation. Il y a toujours des éléments passionnels dans la curiosité. Je vais vous avouer une chose : j'ai une telle passion, une telle boulimie, une telle attirance vers une langue à découvrir que ça peut aller jusqu'à me faire renoncer à une liaison féminine ! Et, dans le cas d'une déception sentimentale, l'aventure d'une langue me console dans les semaines qui suivent. Pas vous ?

808 words

3.5-4.5/1.5 hours

ASSIGNMENT 2 : LEGAL

CANADA

PROVINCE DE QUEBEC
DISTRICT DE MONTREAL

NO :

COUR SUPERIEURE
(Chambre de la famille/Divorce)

LOUISE GILBERT, résidant et domiciliée au 515 rue Hugo, app. 3, dans les ville et district de Montréal, H4N 3F5

Demanderesse

c.

JEAN-LOUIS DUVAL, domicilié et résidant au 15 Ivy Lane, Silver Spring, Maryland, USA. 20902

Défendeur

DECLARATION

Il est déclaré que :

ETAT MATRIMONIAL ET FAMILIAL

1. L'épouse est née à Arthabaska, Paroisse Saints-Martyrs-Canadiens, le 28 décembre, 1960, de l'union de Daniel Gilbert et de Monique Richard. Elle est âgée de 34 ans, le tout tel qu'il appert au certificat de naissance produit sous la cote P-1 ;

2. L'époux est né a New-York, le 26 janvier 1959. Il est le fils de Peter George Duval et de Mary Patricia Dorian. Il est âgé de 35 ans, le tout tel qu'il appert à l'affidavit produit sous la cote P-2 ;

3. Le mariage des parties a été célébré à St-Jérome, Paroisse St-Jérome, le 16 mai 1984, le tout tel qu'il appert au certificat de mariage produit sous la cote P-3 ;

4. Le régime matrimonial alors adopté, au moment de la célébration du mariage, fut le régime de la société d'acquêts, n'ayant pas fait précéder leur union d'un contrat de mariage;

5. Ce régime n'a pas été modifié ;

6. A la date du mariage, l'épouse était célibataire et l'époux était célibataire ;

7. Aucun enfant n'est issu de ce mariage ;

RESIDENCE

8. L'épouse réside habituellement au 515 Hugo, app.3. dans les ville et district de Montréal, et au Québec depuis plus d'un an ;
L'époux réside habituellement au 15 Ivy Lane, Silver Spring,Maryland,USA, 20902;

MOTIFS

9. Il y a échec du mariage pour les motifs suivants :

Les époux ont vécu séparément pendant au moins un an avant le prononcé de la décision sur l'action en divorce et vivaient séparés à la date d'introduction de l'instance ;

RECONCILIATION ET MEDIATION

10. Avant la signature de la présente déclaration :

a) L'avocat de la partie demanderesse a discuté des possibilités de réconciliation et a fourni des renseignements sur les services de consultation ou d'orientation.

b) L'avocat a fourni à la partie demanderesse des renseignements sur les services de médiation susceptibles d'aider à la négociation des points pouvant faire l'objet d'une ordonnance alimentaire ou de garde et a discuté de l'opportunité de négocier ces points ;

MESURES ACCESSOIRES :

11. Aucune mesure accessoire n'est demandée ;

AUTRES PROCEDURES

12. Il n'y a pas eu d'autres procédures d'intentées à l'égard du mariage des parties ;

13. Il n'y a pas de collusion entre les parties ;

PAR CES MOTIFS, PLAISE A CETTE COUR :

PRONONCER un jugement de divorce ;

LE TOUT sans frais, sauf en cas de contestation.

Montréal, ce 28 février 1995

[signature]
LOUISE GILBERT
demanderesse

(signature)
COPIE CONFORME

AVIS A LA PARTIE DEFENDERESSE
RELATIVEMENT A LA CONTESTATION

PRENEZ AVIS que la partie demanderesse a déposé au greffe de la Cour Supérieur du district de Montréal, la présente demande en divorce, et que si vous désirez la contester, vous devrez d'abord comparaître en produisant au greffe du tribunal un acte de comparution sous votre signature ou celle de votre procureur dans les vingt (20) jours de la signification de la demande en divorce ou dans les quarante (40) jours si la signification est faite à l'extérieur du Québec.

Les moyens préliminaires sont proposés et la contestation est produite dans les délais prévus aux articles 813.5 et 813.6 du Code de procédure civile.

PRENEZ DE PLUS AVIS qu'à défaut par vous de comparaître ou de contester dans les délais, la partie demanderesse pourra obtenir contre vous un jugement par défaut.

Montréal, le 28 février 1995

[signature]
St-Jean, Deland & Pasquin
Procureurs de la demanderesse

CERTIFICAT DU GREFFIER

Je, soussigné, greffier pour le district de Montréal atteste qu'il y a eu réception et inscription au greffe de la déclaration en divorce, de l'affidavit de la partie demanderesse, de la déclaration de l'avocat ainsi que de l'avis à la partie défenderesse relativement à la contestation.

Montréal, le 1 mars 1995

JEANNE MONTEUX
GREFFIER

[signature]
COPIE CONFORME

AFFIDAVIT

Je, soussignée, LOUISE GILBERT, résidant et domiciliée au 515 rue Hugo, app. 3, dans les ville et district de Montréal, déclare solennellement ce qui suit :

1. Je suis la demanderesse dans la présente cause ;

2. Tous les faits allégués dans la présente déclaration sont vrais ;

ET J'AI SIGNE :

[signature]
LOUISE GILBERT - demanderesse

Affirmation solennelle reçue et attestée devant moi à Montréal ce 1 mars 1995

[signature]
Commissaire à l'assermentation pour le district de Montréal

DECLARATION DE L'AVOCAT

Je, soussigné, REAL ST-JEAN, avocat du demandeur, atteste que je me suis conformé aux exigences de l'article 9 de la Loi de 1985 sur le divorce.

Montréal, ce 28 février 1995

(signature)
REAL ST-JEAN
Procureur de la demanderesse

(signature)
COPIE CONFORME

688 words

ASSIGNMENT 3 : CHEMICAL

On peut aussi utiliser des composés actifs pâteux comme les dérivés de lanoline (lanoline acétylée) la lanoline et les alcools de lanoline ; les dérivés du cholestérol notamment les esters de cholestérol (12 hydroxie stéarate de cholestéryl) ; les composés pâteux d'origine synthétique; les esters hydroxylés du pentaérythritol (SALACOS 168M), les mono-esters linéaires comme le stéarate de butyle, le propionate d'arachidyle ou l'heptanoate de stéaryle, les triglycérides à chaîne grasse inférieure à C_{16}.

Ces substances sont soit hydrosolubles, soit liposolubles, soit à la fois liposolubles et hydrosolubles soit dispersibles. Elles peuvent être notamment choisies parmi les composés mentionnés dans l'ouvrage précité CTFA aux pages 51 à 101.

L'agent structurant et émulsionnant présent dans la poudre selon l'invention peut être présent en une quantité allant de 4 à 30 % et de préférence en une quantité allant de 4 à 15 % en poids.

Ces composés qui possèdent à la fois les deux propriétés peuvent être choisis parmi les hydrocolloïdes et les biopolymères. Par hydrocolloïdes, on entend des polysaccharides qui peuvent être modifiés notamment par au moins une chaîne hydrophobe.

Par biopolymères, on entend essentiellement les protéines d'origine animale ou végétale et leurs dérivés ou hydrolysats, comme le caséinate de sodium, les protéines de soja, de blé.

La poudre peut contenir un agent de surface mouillant destiné à favoriser la mouillabilité de la poudre lors de la reconstitution de l'émulsion. Cet agent est normalement présent en une quantité allant de 0 à 30 % en poids et mieux de 1 à 20 %. Cet agent de surface permet entre autre, d'augmenter la vitesse de réhydratation de la poudre servant de la dispersion ou émulsion.

Cet agent de surface peut être choisi parmi les agents de surface hydrophiles comme les glycols tels que l'héxylène glycol, le butylène glycol-1,2, la sulfosuccinate d'éthyl-2-hexyle; octylphénol oxyéthyléné (9), les sels des dérivés cocoyle ou lauroyle collagénique, le palmitate de sorbitan et les dérivés polyoxyéthyléné des esters de sorbitan, les sels d'ammonium quaternaire à chaîne grasse.

Le poudre selon l'invention peut aussi comprendre d'autres excipients tels que des colorants, des abrasifs, des opacifiants, des complexants.

Un autre objet de l'invention concerne un procédé de préparation de la poudre telle que définie précédemment.
Ce procédé consiste à former une émulsion huile-dans-eau, à homogénéiser cette émulsion, à déshydrater ladite émulsion pour former ladite poudre.

Selon un mode de réalisation du procédé, l'émulsion utilisée est telle qu'elle a une teneur en matière sèche comprise entre 5 et 70 % en poids et de préférence comprise entre 10 et 60 % en poids. Une telle teneur en matière sèche permet d'avoir une viscosité de l'émulsion telle qu'elle soit suffisamment fluide pour pouvoir être pompée.

Cette teneur en matière sèche donne, dans l'émulsion, une teneur en matière grasse ou en substance cosmétiquement ou dermatologiquement active comprise entre 0,1 et 51 % en poids, et une teneur en agent structurant et émulsionnant comprise entre 0,1
et 18 % en poids.

La phase aqueuse peut être préparée à toute température (0 à 85•C) du moment qu'à la température utilisée, l'agent structurant et émulsionnant soit soluble. On peut travailler à une température comprise entre 40 et 80•C, de manière à avoir une dissolution plus rapide de certains ingrédients.

Il est également possible de préparer le mélange à une température plus basse, d'environ 4 à 10•C, afin de maintenir de bonnes conditions de sécurité bactériologiques.

De manière parallèle, on prépare une phase grasse à la même température que la phase aqueuse, qu'on ajoute à la phase aqueuse en une quantité telle qu'on a, dans l'émulsion qui en résulte, une teneur en matière sèche comprise entre 10 et 60 % en poids.

Ainsi la proportion des constituants telle que définie selon la présente invention garantit une bonne homogénéité et stabilité de l'émulsion, et permet également une excellente reconstitution de l'émulsion.

On forme alors une émulsion en mélangeant lentement les phases aqueuse et grasse, par exemple en incorporant doucement la phase grasse dans la phase aqueuse tout en maintenant une agitation constante et en l'absence de conservateur, une température d'environ 4 à 10•C et à 65 à 75•C environ, toujours pour des raisons bactériologiques.

On obtient ainsi une émulsion huile-dans-eau, présentant un pH dépendant de sa composition, mais généralement compris entre 4 et 9.

Le taux de matière sèche de ladite émulsion est de préférence compris entre 10 et 60 % de manière à permettre le pompage, l'homogénéisation et la déshydratation (ou séchage.)

On homogénéise alors l'émulsion, sous pression élevée, de manière à diminuer la taille moyenne des gouttelettes de la phase grasse jusqu'à environ 1 •m, voire moins. On a observé que l'homogénéisation permet d'améliorer les qualités de réhydratation de la poudre déshydratée, ainsi que ses propriétés fonctionnelles comme, par exemple, l'aptitude à former un gel ferme et stable, ce qui est important dans la cas où l'on souhaite reconstituer un produit ayant l'apparence, la texture et la consistance d'un produit cosmétique d'aspect classique.

On peut employer un homogénéisateur à deux étapes, selon les méthodes habituelles. On peut toutefois prendre la précaution de ne pas dépasser une pression trop élevée, de l'ordre de 350 bars (35 X 10^6 Pa), de manière à éviter une dénaturation de certains agents structurants et émulsionnants qui entraînerait une perte de fonctionnalité et conduirait à une séparation de phases irréversible de l'émulsion. L'homogénéisation peut être effectuée à une température située entre 4 et 45•C, mais préférentiellement entre 4 et 10•C pour des raisons de sécurité bactériologique.

L'émulsion ainsi homogénéisée est alors déshydratée par tout procédé connu, tel que la lyophilisation ou l'atomisation, ou tout autre procédé de séchage sous vide. On obtient une poudre qui peut être éventuellement agglomérée par tout procédé connu. Les températures de l'air chaud utilisé pour le séchage sont de l'ordre de 100 à 160•C et la température de sortie de la poudre est de 30 à 90•C.

917 words

ASSIGNMENT 4 : FINANCE

4-6/2 hours

Faire appel aux marchés financiers internationaux

Plusieurs voies sont possibles pour s'adresser aux marchés financiers internationaux. Dans les pays en développement, les grandes sociétés de services d'utilité publique du secteur privé ont directement accès aux marchés des capitaux d'emprunt et de participation. En octobre 1993, Telecom Argentina a placé une grande partie de son émission d'obligations à sept ans, d'un montant de 500 millions de dollars, auprès d'investisseurs des Etats-Unis et d'Asie, et la société argentine Telefonika s'est adressée, elle aussi, au marché obligataire pour se procurer les fonds nécessaires à son expansion.

L'investissement étranger direct ouvre une autre voie d'accès aux marchés internationaux des capitaux. La General Electric Corporation, qui est un conglomérat international, s'intéresse vivement à la réalisation de projets d'infrastructure dans les pays en développement. Sa filiale, la General Electric Capital Corporation (GECC), émet des titres sur les marchés américains et européens et investit les fonds dans divers projets. En tant qu'investisseur en participation, la GECC a participé, par exemple, à la réalisation, dans le nord de Mindanao, aux Philippines, du projet de construction d'une centrale électrique au diesel de 108 mégawatts. Grâce à l'appui de toutes ses opérations du groupe, le placement des titres émis par la GECC est plus facile que s'il s'agissait uniquement de projets d'équipement électrique pour des pays en développement.

Il est un instrument que l'on utilise beaucoup pour lever des fonds sur le marché financier américain: l'»American Depository Receipt»(ADR). Ce sont des certificats de dépôt qui permettent aux sociétés étrangères de se procurer des fonds sur les marchés américains sans devoir être inscrites à la cote d'une bourse américaine et sans avoir à subir la contrainte des mécanismes complexes de règlement et de transfert. Ils sont émis par une banque dépositaire américaine en contrepartie de titres déposés dans une banque «gardienne» du pays d'origine. En 1990, la Compañía de Teléfonos de Chile (CTC) s'est ainsi procuré 92 millions de dollars à la Bourse de New York par une émission d'actions sous la forme ADR - première grande émission d'actions d'une société latino-américaine depuis 30 ans.

En avril 1990, la U.S. Securities and Exchange Commission a adopté l'Article 144a, qui facilite le placement privé des titres, y compris ceux qui sont placés sous forme d'ADR. Auparavant, les titres émis par placement privé et détenus par des acheteurs qualifiés (établissements gérant un actif d'une valeur minimum de 100 millions de dollars) ne pouvaient être échangés qu'après un délai de conservation de deux ou trois ans. L'Article 144a autorise la mise immédiate des titres sur le marché, sous réserve que le nouvel acheteur soit, lui aussi, qualifié. En outre, après trois ans, les titres peuvent être vendus à n'importe quel acheteur. L'Article 144a a été utilisé en 1992 pour réaliser une émission internationale d'obligations de 207,5 millions de dollars pour la route à péage Mexico-Toluca. Depuis lors, d'autres routes à péage mexicaines et la centrale électrique de la baie de Subic, aux Philippines, ont levé des fonds en utilisant le mécanisme de l'Article 144a.

Au XIXe siècle, déjà

Tout au long du XIXe siècle, alors que l'infrastructure était largement aux mains du secteur privé, les gens se sont plaints que de nombreux projets pourtant utiles étaient négligés faute de moyens de financement. Certaines des plaintes étaient l'expression des difficultés rencontrées pour financer des projets innovateurs dans le secteur des transports (chemins de fer surtout). D'autres poursuivaient un but intéressé : celui de se décharger de tous les risques sur le budget des Etats et, bien souvent, la faillite financière de certaines entreprises a eu des conséquences graves pour les finances de ceux-ci.

Partout dans le monde, les gouvernements ont, sous diverses formes, y compris au moyen de subventions directes, fourni une aide aux projets d'infrastructure du secteur privé. Garanties financières et concessions de terres sont deux moyens toujours d'actualité qui furent utilisés alors.

Garanties. En Inde, si une compagnie ferroviaire n'atteignait pas un taux de rentabilité minimum de 5 %, par exemple, l'Etat comblait l'écart aux termes d'une garantie reposant sur son pouvoir souverain d'imposition. Ce type de garantie a joué également un rôle déterminant dans la construction des chemins de fer canadiens. Mais ces garanties éliminaient les incitations qui auraient encouragé les investisseurs à surveiller la qualité de la gestion, tout en ouvrant la porte à la conclusion d'arrangements «de faveur» entre promoteurs et sociétés de construction et fournisseurs. Parce que beaucoup de projets d'infrastructure étaient uniques en leur genre, la pratique était facile à maquiller. On estime aujourd'hui que les engagements de garantie ont fait monter les coûts de construction.

Concessions de terres. Au cours du XIXe siècle, les terres adjacentes aux voies ferrées et aux canaux ont souvent été cédées à des promoteurs, lesquels ont pu ainsi tirer profit des nombreuses activités commerciales ou industrielles qui ont vu le jour autour de leurs investissements. Fournissant un gage qui pouvait servir à garantir une dette, les dotations foncières ont - comme les garanties d'intérêts - aidé à remédier aux imperfections des marchés financiers. Au Canada, dans les années 1850 et 1860, le non-remboursement des dettes obligataires qu'il avait garanties a opéré une saignée dans les finances de l'Etat. En 1871, la Chambre des communes canadienne a donc adopté une politique de dotation foncière comme moyen de subventionner la construction des chemins de fer sans avoir à alourdir l'impôt. Les dotations foncières se sont révélées particulièrement efficaces dans de vastes opérations spéculatives telles que la construction des chemins de fer indiens et celle des lignes transcontinentales aux Etats-Unis.

Concessions de terres et expropriations

Les concessions de terres se sont révélées être des sûretés efficaces pour des projets innovateurs qui n'auraient peut-être pas pu être financés autrement parce que les prêteurs n'avaient guère l'expérience de telles entreprises. Il existe toutefois un risque que les concessions soient faites en pure perte si elles bénéficient à des projets qui auraient été réalisés de toute manière.

Généralement, cependant, les concessions de terres valent mieux que les garanties d'intérêts car elles représentent une injection de ressources faite une fois pour toutes et ne réduisent pas les incitations à exploiter efficacement le projet. Elles peuvent être un instrument particulièrement bien adapté aux projets très spéculatifs, comme les trains à grande vitesse dans les pays industriels ou les investissements de transports à haut risque dans les pays en développement.

Les concessions de terres soulèvent des questions complexes qui ont trait aux procédures d'acquisition et à l'indemnisation des propriétaires. L'acquisition des terrains peut prendre plusieurs années et retarder considérablement les projets d'infrastructure (certaines des difficultés rencontrées pour la construction du deuxième tronçon de voie express à Bangkok sont dues à des délais de cette nature). Il faut, d'une part, qu'une loi d'expropriation pour cause d'intérêt public définisse de manière appropriée les conditions dans lesquelles les autorités publiques peuvent acquérir les terres ; il faut en outre, comme on l'a vu dans le cas de l'aéroport de Narita, à la périphérie de Tokyo, faire preuve de sensibilité dans l'exécution afin d'éviter les contestations et de coûteux retards.

La perspective d'un rachat de leurs terrains peut inciter les propriétaires à surdévelopper leur bien ou à prendre d'autres mesures pour accroître la valeur de leurs terrains. Une solution pratique consiste à prendre comme norme les prix en vigueur sur le marché et les niveaux de mise en valeur habituels dans les communautés concernées. Le plus difficile est d'indemniser ceux dont les biens se dévaluent parce que la mise en place de nouveaux équipements d'infrastructure modifie l'évolution de l'activité économique. En général, il n'y a pas eu dédommagement pour ce type de perte.

998 words

SECTION 3. TRANSLATIONS OF ASSIGNMENTS AND NOTES

ASSIGNMENT 1: TRANSLATION

What is there to say about Dacian, which the ancestors of the Rumanians spoke before Trajan's troops subjugated them? And what about Pannonian, spoken in the Danube Plain? And Etruscan, in the region of Florence? And Iberian? And Carthaginian? And Ligurian? What can one say about all these languages? Nothing. They are dead. Disappeared. They are enigmas and mysteries. The same is true of Gallic. Contrary to what poorly informed French speakers believe, the number of words whose Gallic etymology turned up in French - out of a total that can be estimated at 40,000 words - does not exceed a hundred! The historian, the medievalist or other scholar, has manuscripts; the geologist can query the rock; the physicist can study gases. But the professional linguist, who ventures into diachrony - in terms of time - has hardly any hope of getting any material that can be handled, any folios or parchment. Memory is his only recourse. Oral transmission. There are oral transmissions that travel through centuries upon centuries. Others do not. But I am not losing any sleep on account of the discovery that it is impossible to exhume a certain past and, hence, a certain piece of knowledge. I am neither gloomy nor pessimistic. But it is only fitting to derive a philosophy for the present and for the future.

You have probably caught on by now, but I will spell it out for you anyway: experience proves that the less one knows about something, the more one believes that one knows about it; and the more one knows about something, the more one realizes how much one does not know. This principle applies perfectly to the linguist in the field, the investigator. And that is due to a very simple numerical and reason: our contemporary world has about 7,000 to 7,500 languages. Those for which we have descriptions, monographs in the form of grammar and vocabulary, account for less than half. The others are not recorded, not known, not described. Moreover, for the most part, these languages of oral tradition are on the way to extinction. Be it Africa -my preferred field of research - or New Guinea, if the linguist does not hurry up with his tape recorder to catch the last phonemes stammered by sick oldsters who no longer speak their language very well because they use it only among themselves - and without ever having passed it on to the young - well, by tomorrow, no trace will be left of that particular language. That introduces the phenomenon of urgency. Motivation enough not to let the shortfall of knowledge get any worse. We devote ourselves to synchronic - horizontal - descriptions of the current structures of language. Our material is alive: it is human beings. But when our source of information does not know - or no longer knows - then one cannot invent in his place.

I experienced the joy of witnessing the birth of a word only once, in 1976, among an African tribe in central Cameroon. Discovering my tape recorder, my source created in his language -called Mbum - the word "talking calabash." The following year, when I returned, the word had been sanctioned and nobody recalled who had invented it. Forgetting the paternity of a word is to be considered as a criterion of its success. I might add that, while linguistics is a science, etymology is not. It is a practice. Nine times out of ten, we do not really know where a word came from.

Against the background of urgency, you will agree, seeking to reconstruct the past is a luxury. Founded on comparatism, starting with languages that are attested to today and looking at common roots, linguistics just the same - with a dose of presumption - has managed to reconstitute some very ancient, unified bases of a good number of our languages. But beyond the ancestral languages, beyond families of languages - Indo-European, Altaic, Sino-Tibetan - there are mysteries. Where does Basque come from? And where did the Basques come from? They were probably the first inhabitants of Europe but their language is not tied to anything, to no family. What, then, is Basque? Well, Basque is Basque: one of the most beautiful enigmas of linguistics.

Linguistics likes to think of itself as a human science and has nothing to do with the field of poetic research. That does not mean that all of theses big question marks, all of these magical, lyrical, and romantic aspects, do not play a major role by way of motivation. There are always elements of passion in curiosity. I grant you one thing: I have such passion, such compulsion, such attraction toward a language that is to be discovered that I might even go so far as to refrain from making love to a woman! And, in case of disappointment in love, the adventure of meeting a language consoles me during the ensuing weeks. You, too?

ASSIGNMENT 1. NOTES

Que dire du dace (line 5) - This text, though dealing with a scholarly subject, is written in a semi-casual, conversational style. A good translation will seek to preserve this style, as the translation of this opening phrase is attempting to do.

Roumains (line 5) - Both Rumanians and Romanians is correct translation. This text mentions several historical people, places and languages. The careful translator will be wise to look up all names where there is the slightest doubt about correct spelling.

francophones mal informés (lines 9) - This phrase has political overtones, which should be carefully weighed when translating it into English so as not to offend French sensibilities.
Nevertheless, the translation has to be accurate, rather than "sanitized."

40 000 mots (line 10) - In English, five-digit numbers require a comma, hence 40,000.

Son unique recours, c'est la mémoire (line 14) - This is an example of changing the order within the sentence. One could translate: "His only recourse is memory." But stylistically, by changing the order of words in the English sentence one often achieves a better flowing sentence, sounding more like English than an English translation of another language. Rearranging a sentence is one of the most important aspects of good translation. (See also lines 15-16).

D'autres, pas (line 15) - Here the comma is not used in translation. Punctuation will differ from one language to the next, because of the different character of each. One should think of punctuation within the context of the target language, not as a direct transfer from the original.

numérique et chiffrée (line 21) - Here the word *chiffrée* is not entirely clear. "ciphered" may or may not be exactly what the author meant. "Calculated" may be better. Or even "tabulated." This is a tough call, so you do the best you can.

phénomène d'urgence (line 38) - Translated here as "the phenomenon of urgency," it may not be the best way to say it in English. "Aspect" or "element" may be better.

paternité (line 34) - This word could be translated as "fathering," "authoring," or any number of similar terms. The choice of the right word in a case like this is not always easy, which is why translation is always challenging.

comparatisme (page 2, line 1) - The translation of this word is a logical replication of the original. This is a linguistic term which does not appear even in major dictionaries, so it may require a little extra research.

attestées (line 1) - "Attested to" is the direct translation of this French word. But somehow one senses that there may be a better way to translate this word.

romanesques (line 10) - Is this word to be translated as "romantic" or "Romanesque"? "Romantic" seems appropriate in this context.

boulimie (line 12) - This is a very descriptive word in French, and perhaps too descriptive in English, where the images it conjures may vitiate the intent of the original. "Compulsion" may not be the best translation, but at least it conveys some of the same idea.

ASSIGNMENT 2: TRANSLATION

CANADA

PROVINCE OF QUEBEC

DISTRICT OF MONTREAL
No:

SUPERIOR COURT
(Family/Divorce Court)

LOUISE GILBERT, residing
at 515 rue Hugo, Apt.3,
in the city and district
of Montreal, H4N 3F5

Plaintiff

Vs.

JEAN-LOUIS DUVAL, residing
at 15 Ivy Lane
Silver Spring,
Maryland, USA 20902

Defendant

STATEMENT

It is stated that:

MARRIAGE AND FAMILY STATUS

1. The wife was born in Arthabaska, Parish of Saints-Martyrs-Canadiens, on December 28, 1960, daughter of Daniel Gilbert and Monique Richard. She is 34 years old, as stated on the birth certificate under classification P-1;

2. The husband was born in New York, on January 26,1959. He is the son of Peter George Duval and Mary Patricia Dorian. He is 35 years old, as stated in the affidavit under classification P-2.

3. The marriage of the parties was celebrated at St-Jérome, Parish of St-Jérome, on May 16, 1984, as stated on the marriage certificate under classification P-3;

4. The marriage settlement adopted then, when their marriage was celebrated, was the community property accrued through acquests only, as they did not enter into a contract;

5. That settlement has not been modified;

6. At the time of the marriage, the wife was single and the husband was single.

7. There have been no children born from this marriage;

RESIDENCE

8. The wife has been residing at 515 Hugo, Apt.3 in the city and district of Montreal, in Quebec for more than one year;

The husband resides at 15 Ivy Lane, Silver Spring, Maryland, USA, 20902;

GROUNDS

9. The marriage fails for the following grounds:

The spouses have lived separately for at least one year prior to the ruling on the divorce proceedings, and lived separately on the date of filing the petition;

RECONCILIATION AND MEDIATION

10. Prior to signing of this statement:

a) The attorney for the plaintiff discussed the possibility of reconciliation and provided information on counseling and guidance services.

b) The attorney provided the plaintiff with information on mediation services that could help in negotiating the possible alimony and custody, and discussed the appropriateness of negotiating these matters;

ANCILLARY COVENANT:

11. No ancillary covenant is requested.

OTHER PROCEEDINGS

12. There have been no other proceedings filed regarding the marriage of the parties;

13. There is no collusion between the parties;

THESE GROUNDS CONSIDERED, WE REQUEST FROM THIS COURT TO:

PRONOUNCE a judgment of divorce;

ALL without costs, except in case of contesting.

Montreal, February 28, 1995

(signature)
LOUISE GILBERT
plaintiff

(signature)
CERTIFIED COPY

NOTICE TO THE DEFENDANT
IN REGARD TO CONTESTING

TAKE NOTICE that the plaintiff has filed at the Court's Clerk's office of the Superior Court of the district of Montreal this petition for divorce, and that if you wish to contest it, you will first have to appear and give the Court's Clerk a Certificate of Appearance bearing your signature or your attorney's within twenty (20) days of the notification of the divorce petition, or within forty (40) days if the notification is made outside of Quebec.

The preliminary means are presented and the dispute is filed within the legal period of time provided for by articles 813.5 and 813.6 of the Civil Proceedings Code.

ALSO TAKE NOTICE that if you fail to appear or contest within the stated period, the plaintiff could obtain a judgment by default against you.

Montreal, February 28, 1995

(signature)
ST-JEAN,DELAND & PASQUIN
Attorneys for the plaintiff

CLERK'S CERTIFICATION

I, the undersigned, Clerk for the District of Montreal, declare that we have received and recorded at the Clerk's Office the declaration of divorce, the plaintiff's affidavit, the attorney's statement, as well as the defendant's notice regarding contesting of same.

Montreal, March 1, 1995

Jeanne Monteux

CLERK (signature)

(signature)
CERTIFIED COPY

AFFIDAVIT

I, the undersigned, LOUISE GILBERT, residing at 515 rue Hugo, Apt.3, in the city and district of Montreal, solemnly declare the following:

1. I am the plaintiff in this matter;

2. All the facts brought forward in this statement are true;

AND I HAVE SIGNED;

(signature)
LOUISE GILBERT - plaintiff

Solemn affirmation received and
witnessed before me in Montreal
on March 1, 1995.

[signature]
Notary Public for the
District of Montreal

ATTORNEY'S STATEMENT

I, the undersigned, REAL ST-JEAN, attorney for the plaintiff, declare that I have conformed to the rules of article 9 of the Divorce Law of 1985.

Montreal, February 28,1995

[signature]
REAL ST-JEAN
Attorney for the plaintiff

[signature]
CERTIFIED COPY

ASSIGNMENT 2: NOTES

General comments:

a. Subject matter

This text represents a specific area of law, namely, civil law as it applies to a divorce case. With this in mind, one should be sensitive to the fact that this original French text, which happens to originate in Canada, reflects Canadian legal terminology in this specific area. The translation is obviously intended for use in the United States, and therefore should reflect American legal usage. Here a good French-English legal dictionary, as well as a basic American legal dictionary (Black's, for instance), would be most useful.

b. Format

We draw your attention to the fact that the original text is not typed in full pages of text, but rather arranged in a very specific format of blocks of text, following, no doubt, a standard Canadian usage. Therefore, the English translation was formatted to look like the original, and each page of translation corresponds exactly to each page of the original. This was done for several good reasons: (a) an end-user of a translation would often need to compare the two texts, and this exact replication makes it very easy to compare, and also to make sure nothing is missing; (b) it helps the translator to check his/her own work, making sure nothing was left out; and (c) it conveys the sense of orderliness and accuracy which is critical in legal documents.

COUR SUPERIEURE (line 3) - The names of courts, legal office, and other legal bodies and persons differ from country to country. It is not always possible to convey the exact meaning of those terms by simply providing a direct translation, which at times may require a Translator's note attached to the document.

résidant et domiciliée (lines 7-8) - This is translated as "residing" (even this word is superfluous in American legal usage, where normally only the name and address are provided). Here is an example of official legal language, where it may or may not be necessary to translate word for word.

Défendeur (line 19) - While "defendant" is used in English in both civil and criminal cases, in French the term is *défendeur* for a civil case and *accusé* for a criminal one. This is a clear example of the care one must take in handling legal terminology, which often does not translate directly.

Paroisse (line 25) - This is a religious territorial term, translated as "parish." Territorial terms, such as county, district, state and so on also require special attention, since they vary from one country to the next. If in doubt about a territorial or geographical term, check it carefully to make sure you are using the correct term.

régime matrimonial (line 34) - This is a Canadian legal term which does not directly correspond to an

American equivalent.

régime de la société d'acquêts (lines 34-35) - Legal term.

CONTESTATION (page 3, line 11) - Contesting, or the right to contest, or dispute.

Additional observations:

Since legal documents such as a petition for divorce contain a fairly standard text, you may want to get hold of one or more texts of English-language petitions for divorce, to familiarize yourself with the style and terminology. Clearly, one does not always have the time and means to obtain this kind of information, but if this is a subject you expect to translate fairly regularly, it is worth the effort.

Also, it is important to know the purpose of a particular translation, although a translator is not always given this information by the client. If it is to be used in court, it has to be accurate to the point of being accepted as admissible evidence. On the other hand, if it is only for information purposes - say the defendant in this case wanted to see a copy in English since he does not read French, then you need not spend nearly as much time and effort to make sure every single word is the best possible equivalent of the original.

ASSIGNMENT 3: TRANSLATION

We can also use pasty active compounds like lanolin by-products (acetyl lanolin), lanolin, and lanolin alcohols; cholesterol by-products, like cholesterol esters (12 cholesteryl hydroxy stearate); pasty compounds of synthetic origin; pentaerythritol hydroxylated esters (SALACOS 168M), linear mono-esters like butyl stearate, arachidyle propionate or stearyl heptanoate, triglycerides with a fatty chain inferior to C_{16}.

These substances are either hydrosoluble, liposoluble, or liposoluble and hydrosoluble at the same time, or dispersible. They can be chosen among the compounds that are in the book mentioned in pages 51 to 101.

The structuring and emulsifying agent that is present in the powder according to this invention can be present in a quantity that can be from 4 to 30%, and preferably from 4 to 15% in weight.

These compounds which at one time possess the two properties can be chosen from among the hydro-colloids and the biopolymers. By hydro-colloids, we mean polysaccharides which can be modified especially by a less hydrophobic chain.

When we mention biopolymers, we essentially mean proteins of animal or vegetable origin and their by-products, or hydrolysates, like sodium caseinate, and soy and wheat proteins.

The powder can contain a surface wetting agent that would increase the wettability of the powder when the reconstruction of the emulsion takes place. This agent is generally present in an amount that goes from 0 to 30% in weight, and better from 1 to 20%. This surface agent especially allows the increase of the speed of rehydration of the powder using the dispersion or emulsion.

This surface agent can be chosen among the hydrophile surface agents, like glycols, such as hexylene glycol, 1,2-butylene glycol, 2-ethylhexyl sulfosuccinate; oxyethylene octylphenol (9), and the salts derived from cocoyle and collagenic lauroyl, sorbitan palpitate, and the polyoxyethylene by-products of sorbitate palmitate esters, salts of fatty chain quaternary ammonium.

According to this invention, the powder can contain other excipients such as colorants, abrasives, opacifiants and complexants.

Another matter relating to this invention relates to the preparation process for the powder as we have described it.

This process consists of making an oil-in-water emulsion, in homogenizing this emulsion, and in dehydrating said emulsion to make said powder.

According to the way this process is performed, the emulsion that is used is such that it has a dry matter that is between 5 and 70% in weight, and preferably between 10 and 60% in weight. Such an amount of dry matter allows obtaining an emulsion with a viscosity such that it is sufficiently fluid to be pumped.

The content of dry matter gives, in the emulsion, a content of fat or of a cosmetically or dermatologically active substance between 0.1 and 51% in weight, and a content of structuring and emulsifying agent between 0.1 and 18% in weight.

The aqueous phase can be prepared at all temperatures (0 to 85•C) provided that the structuring and emulsifying agent is soluble at the temperature being used. It is possible to work at a temperature between 40 and 80•C in order to obtain a quicker solution of certain ingredients.

It is possible as well to prepare the mixture at a lower temperature, around 4 to 10•C, in order to maintain good bacteriologic security conditions.

In a parallel manner, we can prepare a fat phase at the same temperature as the aqueous phase, that we add to the aqueous phase in such a quantity so that we have, in the resulting emulsion, a content of dry matter that is between 10 and 60% in weight.

Thus a proportion of the constituents as it is defined according to this invention guarantees the emulsion with a good homogeneity and stability, and also allows an excellent reconstitution of the emulsion.

We then make an emulsion by slowly mixing the fat and aqueous phases, for example by slowly incorporating the fat phase into the aqueous phase and maintaining a constant agitation, and, in the absence of a preservative agent, a temperature around 4 to 10•C and 65 to 75•C, again for bacteriological reasons.

We then obtain an oil-in-water emulsion, offering a pH depending on its composition, but generally between 4 and 9.

The percentage of dry matter of said emulsion is preferably between 10 and 60%, in order to allow the pumping, the homogenization and the dehydration (or drying).

We then homogenize the emulsion, under high pressure, in order to reduce the average size of the droplets of the fatty phase down to about 1μm, or less. We have observed that the homogenization improves the qualities of rehydration of the dehydrated powder, a well as its functional characteristics, such as, for instance, the ability to form a firm and stable gel, which is important in an instance when we want to reconstitute a product that would have the appearance, texture and consistency of a cosmetic product with classic features.

A two stage homogenizer can be used, according to standard methods. However, we should be careful not to use too high a pressure, around 350 bars (35 X 10^6 Pa), in order to avoid any denaturation of certain structuring or emulsifying agents which would trigger a loss of functionality and would lead to the irreversible separation of the phases of the emulsion. The homogenization can be performed at a temperature between 4 and 45•C, for reasons of bacteriological security.

The homogenized emulsion is then dehydrated by any known procedure, like lyophilization or atomization, or any other drying process in a vacuum. We obtain a powder that eventually can be compressed by any known method. The temperature of the hot air that is used for the drying process is around 100 to 160•C and the temperature for removing the powder is between 30 and 90•C.

ASSIGNMENT 3: NOTES

General comments:

a. Subject matter

Though this particular assignment presents many examples of specific terminology, the text itself is straightforward, and presents no real difficulty in terms of sentence structure or language style. Unless one is thoroughly familiar with the chemical terms in this text, it would be best not to start translating right away, but first to make a list of all the chemical terms in the text one is not certain of.

b. References

A good chemical dictionary should have all or nearly all the technical terms of this text. If, after thorough consultation with such a source you still have an unknown term, the next thing to do is call someone with an appropriate chemical background.

Bear in mind that exact sciences such as chemistry have a well-defined and fairly limited vocabulary. After doing this kind of an assignment several times you will be able to do it much faster and with minimal time spent on research.

On peut utiliser (line 3) - The French style of chemical writing is impersonal, while the English translation is in the first person plural. It could have also been translated as "One can" instead of "We can." In English, however, which is a less abstract language than French, using a pesonalized style makes reading easier.

(lanoline acétylée) la lanoline (line 3) - there is no comma in the original after the parenthesis, although it is quite clear that a comma is required. In a case as simple and clear-cut as this, the translator puts a comma in the translation without the need for any explanations (except for a special situation where such action is required).

synthétique: (line 5) - here a semicolon was replaced by a colon. See previous note.

CTFA (line 11) - Here the reference is not explained.

ASSIGNMENT 4: TRANSLATION

Tapping international capital markets

Several channels exist for tapping international capital markets. The larger private utilities in developing countries have direct access to debt and equity markets. In October 1993 Telecom Argentina placed much of its $500 million, seven-year bond issue with U.S. and Asian investors; Argentina's Telefonika has also used bond market placements to raise expansion funds.

Foreign direct investment opens another route into international equity markets. General Electric Corporation, an international conglomerate, has an active interest in developing infrastructure projects in developing countries. Its subsidiary, the General Electric Capital Corporation (GECC), issues securities on U.S. and European markets and invests the funds in selected projects. GECC has participated as an equity investor, for instance, in the Northern Mindanao power project - a 108-megawatt diesel-fired power project in the Philippines. Backed by the group's total operations, the placement of securities issued by GECC is easier than it would be for developing country power projects alone.

An instrument widely used to tap resources in the U.S. capital market is the American depositary receipt (ADR). ADRs are certificates of deposit that enable foreign companies to raise equity on U.S. markets without the need for a listing on a U.S. stock exchange and without complex settlement and transfer mechanisms. They are issued by a U.S. depository bank, and the underlying shares of the company are held in trust by a custodian bank in the home country. In 1990 Compañía de Teléfonos de Chile (CTC) raised $92 million on the New York Stock Exchange through an issue of equity in the form of ADRs - the first major equity issue from Latin America in three decades.

In April 1990 the U.S. Securities and Exchange Commission approved rule 144a, facilitating private placement of securities, including those placed as ADRs. Before then, privately placed securities held by qualified buyers (institutions that manage assets worth at least $100 million) could be traded only after a two- or three-year holding period. Rule 144a allows trading to occur immediately, provided that the new buyer is also qualified. Moreover, after three years the securities can be sold to all buyers. Rule 144a was used in 1992 to enable a $207.5 million international bond issue for the Mexico City-Toluca Toll Road. Since then, other Mexican toll roads and the Subic Bay power plant in the Philippines have raised funds using rule 144a.

Warning signs from the nineteenth century

Throughout the nineteenth century, when infrastructure was largely in private hands, contemporaries complained that many worthwhile projects were neglected for lack of financing. Some of the complaints reflected the difficulties of financing pioneering transportation (especially railway) projects. Other complaints were self-serving efforts to shift all risk on to government budgets, and in many cases the financial bankruptcy of enterprises had severe consequences for government finances.

Governments all over the world provided aid to private infrastructure projects in various forms, including direct subsidies. Two instruments in use then and of current interest as well are financial guarantees and land grants.

Guarantees. In India, if a railway company did not attain a minimum rate of return of, for example, 5 percent, the government made up the difference under the terms of a guarantee backed by its full powers of taxation. Such guarantees were also critical in the construction of the Canadian railways. But guarantees removed incentives for investors to monitor management performance while opening the way for promoters to negotiate so-called "sweetheart" deals with construction and supply companies. Because many infrastructure projects were one of a kind, the practice could be readily disguised. It now appears that bond guarantees led to higher construction costs.

Land grants. During the nineteenth century, lands adjoining railways and canals were often ceded to promoters, allowing them to profit from the many side businesses that grew up around their investments. By providing collateral that could be used to back bonded debt, land grants - like interest guarantees - corrected for capital market imperfections. In Canada during the 1850s and 1860s, defaults on guaranteed bonds drained government revenues. In 1871, therefore, the Canadian House of Commons adopted a policy of land grants as a way to subsidize railway construction without having to raise the rate of taxation. Land grants proved most effective in such large speculative ventures as the Indian railroads and the transcontinental lines in the United States.

Land grants and eminent domain

Land grants have proved to be a valuable form of collateral for innovative projects that might otherwise not have been financed because lenders had little experience with similar projects. But in implementing a policy of land grants, there is a risk that the grants might be wasted if they are given to projects that would be built in any case.

Overall, however, land grants have greater merit than interest guarantees because they represent a one-time infusion of resources and do not reduce the incentives for efficient operation of the project. They may be especially suited for more speculative projects - such as high-speed rail in industrial countries or high-risk transport investment in developing countries.

Awarding land grants raises complex questions about acquisition procedures and compensation of landholders. Land acquisition can take several years and delay infrastructure projects substantially - some of the difficulties of the Second Stage Expressway in Bangkok are related to these delays. Not only is an appropriate law of eminent domain required to define the terms under which the government can acquire the land, but, as was demonstrated in the case of Narita Airport outside Tokyo, lack of sensitivity in implementation can lead to contentious and expensive delays.

In anticipation of land being acquired, landowners have an incentive to overdevelop their property or undertake other measures to overvalue their land. A practical solution is to use prevailing market prices and community standards of land development as a norm. The more difficult issue is one of compensating those whose property values fall as the flow of business activity changes because of new infrastructure development. In general, governments have not compensated such losses.

ASSIGNMENT 4: NOTES

General comments:

a. Financial Translation

In translation, there is a basic difference between translating financial subjects and other technical subjects, such as legal or medical. While it is relatively easy to master the methodology of working with most technical vocabularies - even if one does not have the technical or professional background of the particular field in which one translates - in financial subjects it is necessary to have at least a general knowledge of the subject. This may be due to the fact that financial terminology and concepts are not always as readily translatable as as other technical subjects. The upshot of all this is that one should not be hasty to accept a financial translation assignment if one does not work in this field on a regular basis.

b. Subject matter

This particular assignment consists of three texts derived from a publication of an international financial organization. As with most major organizations and corporations, this organization has its own so-called "corporate style," which affects the way this material is translated. Normally, an organization of this magnitude employs its own translators, or uses outside translators on a regular basis, to acquaint them with its style If called upon to translate this kind of text, be sure to familiarize yourself with the organization's style.

marchés des capitaux d'emprunt et de participation (line 6) - "Debt and equity markets" are seemingly simple terms, yet they represent financial/economic terminology which must be followed carefully and accurately. If in doubt, consult financial or economic dictionaries. Better yet, get in touch with someone who works in this field and knows the current terms used.

500 millions de dollars (line 7-8) - The rendering of currency numbers and symbols is a critical aspect of financial translation. While the English translation uses the American dollar sign, the French spells out the words. Another international way of referring to U.S. currency is US$500 million, to distinguish it from other currencies.

La General Electric Corporation (line 10) - The name of a company is not translated from the original language, unless it is known by an equivalent name in the country of the target language.

GECC (line 13) - Here the acronym reflects the original English name, rather than a French equivalent. This will only vary if the company or organization in question has French equivalent acronym, such as OTAN (or Otan) for NATO, for example. (See also ADR, as well as CTC, which stands for a Spanish company name).

une banque "gardienne" (line 24) - the placing of the French word between quotation marks indicates that this is not a usual French financial term. "Custodian bank," on the other hand, is a common American financial term, therefore there is no need for quotation marks.

207,5 millions (line 34) - The European use of comma is replaced by the American use of period for decimals.

"de faveur" (page 2, line 17) - Here both the French and the English equivalent, "'sweetheart' deals" are given between quotation marks, since both are colloquial, semi-informal, rather than formal financial terms.

SECTION 4

WHERE DO I GO FROM HERE?

After you have completed all the assignments, or at least those you have chosen to do, you have to make a major decision. If you have never translated for profit before, you have to ask yourself if you are ready to try your hand at soliciting for-profit translation work. If the answer is yes, turn to the book in this Kit, *Guide for Translators,* and read Chapters 9 and 10, on how to operate successfully as a freelance translator, and where to find work. If you have translated for profit before in a specific area, such as legal documents, and you feel you are now ready to venture into another area, such as medical translation, first try out some short assignments in that field, until you become comfortable with it.

In either case, the next step is to turn to Appendix 3 in the book, and look up sources of translation work. We urge you to develop a relationship with one or more translation companies in your own geographical area. There is absolutely no reason in this day and age for a translator, say, in Wisconsin, not to develop a profitable relationship with a translation company in Florida, and in time you may indeed find out that a certain company on the other side of the continent is your best source of work. But as a beginner, there are many advantages to interfacing personally with the staff of a translation company close to home. They can give you a great deal of practical advice, help you with the hardware and the software, and share other kinds of experience with you. There is an old saying: A good neighbor is better than a distant relative.

If, on the other hand, you feel you are not ready to take the plunge, you may want to consider a translation course or study program. Refer to Appendix 4 in the book, and see if there is a program close to home you can sign up for. Or you may decide to continue practicing on your own.

Whatever you decide to do, don't give up too easily. If you do enjoy the challenge of translation, continue to improve you skills. Remember: Translation can be a full-time career or a very fulfilling and profitable sideline. It is definitely the kind of expertise worth having, no matter what else you choose to do with your time.

Order Form

or **e-mail** to Language@SchreiberLanguage.com
or **mail** to: **Schreiber Publishing**, PO Box 4193 Rockville, MD 20849
USA or **call** toll free 1-800-296-1961 (in Maryland 301-589-5831)
or visit our website: **www.SchreiberLanguage.com**

____ copies of ***The Translator's Handbook*** 8th Revised Ed. $25.95 $ ____ $ ____

____ copies of ***Spanish Business Dictionary*** 3rd Edition. $24.95 $ ____

____ copies of ***Multicultural Spanish Dictionary, 2nd Ed*** $24.95 $ ____

____ copies of ***Translator Self-Training*** $69.00 Circle language(s):

Spanish French German Russian Japanese Chinese Portuguese Italian Arabic Hebrew $ ____

____ copies of ***Translator Self-Training - Spanish Medical*** $69.00 $ ____

____ copies of ***Translator Self-Training - Spanish Legal*** $69.00 $ ____

sub-total $ ____

Maryland residents add 6% sales tax to sub-total $ ____

In the U.S. add $4.50 for shipping/handling per single copy and $2.00 for each additional book. Overseas add US$9 for one book, and $5 for each additional book (for books priced under $50), or $18 per book priced over $50 $____

Order total $ ======

Please charge my • Visa, • MasterCard; • Check or money order enclosed.

Name ________________ Phone ________________ E-mail ________________

Address ________________ City ________________ State____ Zip ________

Card No. ________ ________ ________ ________ Exp. date (month) ___ (year) ___